Beyond Registration

Beyond Registration

Getting the best from **ISO 9001** and **business improvement**

Steve Tanner, EC*for*BE

with

Mike Bailey and Charles Pertwee, BSI

First published 2002
This edition published 2003

Prepared by The European Centre *for* Business Excellence
Various terms in this work are copyright and/or trademarks of their owners in various territories.
All copyrights are acknowledged: trademarks are used for discussion purposes and their use is not
intended to imply ownership.

© BSI 2003

ISBN 0 580 42589 4

BSI reference: BIP 2020

A catalogue record for this book is available from the British Library.

Typeset by Monolith – www.monolith.uk.com
Printed by MPG Books Ltd, Bodmin, Cornwall

Contents

Contents

Foreword

Over several decades quality standards have been used to improve the quality of products and services as competition for market share, from home and overseas, increased. More recently, the drive to improve the levels of service offered by the public sector has seen the adoption of quality standards as a step towards the goal of excellence in those organizations. As a consequence the number of companies and organizations seeking certification to quality standards continues to grow.

Since the early 1990s, quality and 'excellence' models have been developed throughout the world, the most popular being the Deming Prize in Japan, the American Baldrige Award framework and, in Europe, the EFQM Excellence Model®. Like the ISO 9000:2000 quality management standard, the aim of these frameworks is to improve organizational capability and the results they obtain. *Beyond Registration* is one of the few publications that provides a comparison of some of these frameworks, side by side, showing how they support each other.

Organizations are often faced with a bewildering range of quality tools and techniques, all with their unique features, to use on their quality journey. *Beyond Registration* summarizes over 20 improvement approaches and, in particular, provides guidance on how they can be used to support an improvement in results, from the platform of an ISO 9000:2000 based management system.

Beyond Registration is a collaborative project between BSI and the European Centre *for* Business Excellence and provides an extremely valuable resource that should help all types of organizations to improve their performance.

Professor John Oakland
Leeds University Business School

Introduction

Many organizations aim for world-class performance. The tools they can use to get there – business improvement models and approaches – are the subject of this book.

Business improvement *models* cover an organization's activities, and when implemented can lead to world-class performance. Business improvement *approaches* are applied to specific tasks, outputs or areas of activity, and are the building blocks of world-class performance.

Business improvement models evaluate and recognize 'world class' performance; the most popular are ISO 9001, the EFQM Excellence Model® and the American Baldrige Model. Business improvement approaches include ongoing programmes of improvement such as Total Quality Management, BPIR or Six Sigma, and tools that help managers understand the business, such as Balanced Scorecards and the Process Classification Framework.

There is an overlap between business improvement models and business improvement approaches. The differences between them are:

Improvement model	Improvement approach
Designed to be holistic covering all the organization's activities	Designed for a specific task or area of activity with an organization
May be used to determine actions as well as providing measurement	Product-based and often subject to a lifecycle
Owned by a recognized body, such as EFQM	Related to particular 'schools' such as consultancies or business books
Many role model organizations	Limited role model organizations
Used as a basis of an award process	In some cases used as a basis of an award in the subject area
Leads to 'world-class' performance	A building block of 'world-class' performance

About this book

Beyond Registration is for all organizations seeking continuous improvement and will be particularly relevant to enterprises that have registered to ISO 9001 and are looking for ways forward.

Beyond Registration will help organizations improve their performance. It outlines several business improvement models and approaches, and compares them with ISO 9001. It demonstrates how ISO 9001 provides support to and is consistent with those models and approaches.

Part 1 discusses the Baldrige and EFQM Excellence Models®. ISO 9001 can be the starting point for the journey towards world-class performance. It provides the platform for taking the organization forward by achieving control over leadership, customer focus and continuous improvement. Comparison tables show how the Baldrige and EFQM Excellence Models® build on the foundations laid by ISO 9001 and indicate potential areas for improvement once registration to ISO 9001 has been achieved.

Part 2 describes leading business improvement approaches and shows how they can deliver improvement. The application, background, principles and methods of each approach are covered, and the relationship with ISO 9001 shown.

A glossary explains the terms and abbreviations used in the book, and tables in Appendix 1 show where the business improvement approaches can be used to support the requirements of ISO 9001, Baldrige and the EFQM Excellence Model®. Sources of further information can be found in Appendix 2, and Appendix 3 gives details on the European Centre *for* Business Excellence and BSI Management Systems.

Part 1: ISO 9001 and the business improvement models

The ISO 9001 Quality System

Background

The 1980s witnessed an increased use of formal quality management systems amongst business communities around the world. BS 5750 was introduced in 1979 as the standard for quality assurance and was used by organizations as a means to increase accuracy, efficiency and, as a result, competitiveness. Following a revision in 1987, ISO 9001 was issued as an international standard in 1994. The standard has evolved towards a total quality approach and the 2000 version shifts the emphasis to the enhancement of customer satisfaction through 'continual improvement'. During its evolution the standard has become a benchmark and, in many cases, the entry criterion for suppliers.

Many organizations have adopted ISO 9001 as a basis for their management system, and a recent study conducted by the European Centre *for* Business Excellence confirmed that adoption had brought many benefits. The study examined the reasons for adoption and found that the commonest was that customers required it. In one case this led to an additional $6m of sales, and in another case an additional £15m. The second most common reason for adoption was the trend in the marketplace; there was a feeling that organizations which achieved registration would have a competitive advantage.

Many organizations, however, have implemented ISO 9001 for the operational advantages that it delivers. One organization researched for the European Centre *for* Business Excellence study attributed £2.9m savings to the adoption of ISO 9001. This trend is expected to grow as the full benefits of the new standard are realized.

Principles

ISO 9001 identifies eight quality management principles that can be used by top management to lead the organization towards improved performance:

1. customer focus;
2. leadership;
3. involvement of people;
4. process approach;
5. systems approach to management;
6. continual improvement;
7. factual approach to decision making;
8. mutually beneficial supplier relationships.

There is a close match between these principles and the principles that underpin the two business improvement models described in the next section. The Baldrige model has its core values and concepts, and the EFQM Excellence Model its fundamental concepts of excellence.

Structure

ISO 9001 has a structure with five main requirements:

1. quality management system;
2. management responsibility;
3. resource management;
4. product realization;
5. measurement, analysis and improvement.

It can be represented like this:

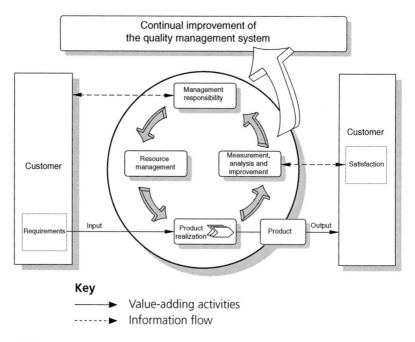

Key

——————▶ Value-adding activities

------▶ Information flow

source: ISO 9001: 2000

Application

ISO 9001 focuses on the identification and control of processes. Once the processes of a management system have been determined Deming's plan-do-check-act cycle can be applied to the processes to seek continual improvement. (See 'Kaizen/Continuous Improvement' on page 55 for more on Deming's cycle of improvement.)

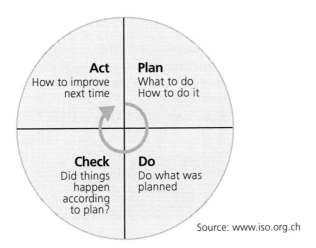

Source: www.iso.org.ch

One significant difference between the application of the new standard and the previous version is in the way that third party assessments are conducted. Under the previous standard there was a risk that an assessment would only focus on a comparison between the detail presented within a series of documented procedures and the activities observed in an organization.

Procedure*
'Specified way to carry out an activity or a process' – may be documented or not

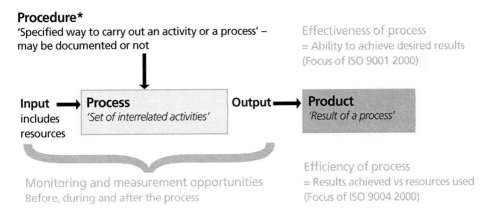

This is the definition of 'procedure' given in ISO 9000 2000. This does not necessarily mean one of the six 'documented procedures' required by ISO 9001 2000 source: www.iso.org.ch

The assessment approach required for ISO 9001:2000 is focused on the need to identify the processes within the organization that contribute to the enhancement of the satisfaction of its customers. Once established, the assessors then need to test these processes to ensure that they are integrated and effective. This has changed assessments from being 'conformance' audits to being value-adding assessments.

Improvement is achieved through the analysis of factual data:

- objectives establish a focus for the achievement of goals;
- corrective action systems analyse the root causes of problems and prevent recurrence;
- preventive action systems provide the framework with a risk or loss management tool by identifying and preventing potential problems;
- analysis of data generated through monitoring and measuring activities identifies and/or confirms improvement.

Integration of ISO 9001 with actual business practice relies upon an organization's top management becoming the owners of their improvement system. The standard then provides the framework to control and improve the organization's processes relating to human resources, infrastructure, environment, product or service delivery and measurement.

When used in the spirit intended, ISO 9001 is an excellent control and improvement tool. This 'spirit' has been captured within the eight quality management principles. It ensures that improvement 'gains' are sustained. It will directly drive breakthrough improvement and has structured linkages to 'best practice' approaches to improvement.

Like any framework, ISO 9001 can be used inappropriately. For optimal effect it needs to be implemented with a view to excellence rather than compliance; only then will it work for the business rather than making extra work for it.

Key strengths of ISO 9001

- focuses on customers' needs;
- avoids improvization and lack of control;
- both process and performance focused;
- sustainable improvement;
- the accepted world quality management standard.

Well-known Business Models

This section discusses two business improvement models: the Baldrige model and the EFQM Excellence Model®. The Baldrige model forms the basis of the US award process and is used in many parts of the world heavily influenced by the USA, such as the Middle East. There are also a number of State Awards at a more local level.

The European Foundation for Quality Management (EFQM) Excellence Model, which is used across Europe, is similar to the Baldrige model, and is used as the basis of the annual European Quality Award as well as National Quality Awards in European countries. Within European countries, there are often Regional Awards to support the achievement of excellence within geographical regions.

There are other business improvement models from around the world that have not been included here, notably Japan's Deming Prize. This was the first major business improvement framework to be developed and all the others have their roots in this model. The assessment criteria are kept confidential and have not been translated from the original Japanese, so detailed comparisons are difficult. This model has undergone some revision over the years and now has adopted some of the concepts of the EFQM Excellence Model and Baldrige model, such as the focus on sustainability.

The Malcolm Baldrige Award

Background

The Malcolm Baldrige National Quality Award was created by Public Law in 1987 and led to the creation of a new partnership between government and the private sector aimed at promoting business excellence. The model has three important roles in strengthening US competitiveness:

1. to help improve organizational performance practices, capabilities, and results;
2. to facilitate communication and sharing of best practices information among US organizations of all types;
3. to serve as a working tool for understanding and managing performance and for guiding planning and opportunities for learning.

Although originally only for private organizations, the guidelines have been extended to public and voluntary organizations, such as health and education. The popularity of the model within America is so great that although there are only around 30-50 applications for the award every year, over 250,000 organizations request copies of the guidelines.

As the Baldrige Award is now well established, researchers have been observing the benefits of the application of the model to organizations. In a recent study, Hendricks and Singhal (1999) concluded that business excellence 'pays off handsomely' and is a source of competitive advantage. It was noted, however, that it is not a replacement for corporate strategy or a guarantee for success.

Core values and concepts

The model is built upon the following set of interrelated core values and concepts:

- visionary leadership;
- customer-driven excellence;
- organizational and personal learning;
- valuing employees and partners;
- agility;
- focus on the future;
- managing for innovation;
- management by fact;
- social responsibility;
- focus on results and creating value;
- systems perspective.

These values and concepts are embedded beliefs and behaviours found in high-performing organizations. They are the foundation for integrating key business requirements into a results-oriented framework that creates a basis for action and feedback.

Structure

The 2003 Baldrige Award criteria framework consists of seven categories:

1. leadership;
2. strategic planning;
3. customer and market focus;
4. measurement, analysis and knowledge management;
5. human resource focus;
6. process management;
7. business results.

The structure can be represented as follows:

source: Baldrige 2003 Guidelines

Application

Each of the seven categories is broken down into 18 items. Organizations applying the framework first identify the activities they undertake and then review these against the requirements of each item. This review is termed a 'self-assessment'.

- The *strengths and areas for improvement* for each item are noted. A number of *areas to address* aid this analysis.
- A score out of a maximum of 100 per cent is based on two classifications. These are: *approach-deployment* and *results*.
- Categories 1–6 are scored against *approach-deployment* and category 7, business results, is scored against *results*.
- An overall score is calculated for each of the seven categories, which are then weighted to calculate a score out of 1,000 points. Categories 1–6 carry 55 per cent of the weighting.

Organizations at the start of the quality journey will typically score less than 250 points whereas 'world-class' organizations would score over 800 points.

There are many ways to conduct the self-assessment, from a simple review undertaken by a team of people to the collation of a 75-page report assessed by an independent team. All approaches have their positive and negative points, but it is generally accepted that the production of the report and the use of an assessment team (the approach used in applications for the Baldrige Award) give the most accurate results and quality feedback.

Key strengths of the Baldrige model

- strong customer/market focus and strategy focus;
- people and process focus;
- integrated systems approach;
- fact-based systems for improving performance;
- focus on results.

The EFQM Excellence Model®

Background

The European Foundation for Quality Management (EFQM) was founded by 14 chief executives of leading European companies with the objective of enhancing the competitive position of European organizations in the world market. The aims are to:

- stimulate and assist organizations throughout Europe to participate in improvement activities leading ultimately to excellence in customer satisfaction, employee satisfaction, impact on society and business results; and
- support the managers of European organizations in accelerating the process of making Total Quality Management a decisive factor for achieving global competitive advantage.

The European Model for Total Quality was launched by EFQM in 1991, with the first European Quality Award and European Quality Prizes given in 1992. Since its launch the model has evolved and is now known as the EFQM Excellence Model®.

Research has been conducted into the reasons why organizations adopt the EFQM Excellence Model® and the benefits it brings. Reed (1995) concluded that public sector organizations used it primarily to measure success and implement best practice. Another study (ECforBE, 1997) suggested that the main reasons for commencing self-assessment are to:

- provide a driver for continuous improvement;
- identify an organization's areas for improvement;
- increase total quality awareness throughout the organization;
- increase the commitment of line management to TQM.

The X Factor, a research report published by the British Quality Foundation in 1998, made a major contribution to the understanding of the benefits of business excellence to organizations. The research included a review of the submission documents of award-winning organizations and four in-depth case studies, and demonstrated that European and UK award-winning organizations show strong positive trends across a range of financial measures over both three and five year periods, even if their performance against their own targets was less satisfactory.

Principles

Truly excellent organizations are measured by their ability to achieve and sustain outstanding results for all their stakeholders – customers, employees, shareholders and the community. This requires a management approach based on eight fundamental concepts:

1. results orientation;
2. customer focus;

3. leadership and constancy of purpose;
4. management by process and facts;
5. people development and involvement;
6. continuous learning, innovation and improvement;
7. partnership development;
8. corporate social responsibility.

Structure

The EFQM Excellence Model consists of five enabler criteria:

1. leadership;
2. policy and strategy;
3. people;
4. partnerships and resources;
5. processes;

and four results criteria:

1. customer results;
2. people results;
3. society results;
4. key performance results.

The structure can be represented as follows:

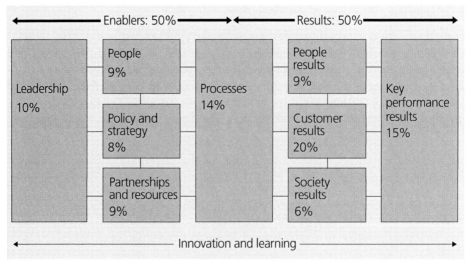

®1999–2003 EFQM. The Model is a registered trademark of the EFQM

Application

The application of the EFQM Excellence Model is similar to that of the Baldrige model. Each criterion is broken down into a number of criteria parts and each of these has a number of supporting guidance points.

However, the two approaches do vary significantly in their approach to scoring. The EFQM Excellence Model makes use of a 'Plan – Do – Check – Act' approach entitled RADAR:

- Results
- Approach
- Deployment
- Assessment and Review.

Like the Baldrige model, there are two elements to the scoring, enablers and results, but unlike the Baldrige model, within each criteria all the criteria parts carry the same weight:

- an overall score is calculated for each of the nine criteria;
- the criteria are then weighted to calculate a score out of 1,000 points;
- 50 per cent of the total weighting is given to the enabler criteria and 50 per cent to the results. (For the Baldrige model this ratio is 55:45 per cent in favour of the enabler equivalent.)

Organizations at the start of the quality journey will typically score less than 250 points out of 1,000, whereas 'world-class' organizations winning the European Award would score over 800 points.

Key strengths of the EFQM Excellence Model

- strong business focus and emphasis on business results;
- balanced scorecard performance tracking and results;
- first framework to introduce 'impact on society' concept;
- enabler-result structure encourages understanding of cause and effect;
- holistic business excellence model.

Linkages

ISO 9001 has strong linkages to the EFQM Excellence Model and the Baldrige model, so an organization can use its ISO 9001 registered quality manual as a source of approaches to populate the models.

Example: Linking the EFQM Excellence Model and ISO 9001

If a business wanted to self-assess against the EFQM Excellence Model it could do so against its own application of ISO 9001. Criterion 1 on 'Leadership', for example, can be linked to section 5 'Management responsibility' in ISO 9001. At a lower level, criterion part 1a 'Leaders develop the mission, vision, values and ethics and are role models of a culture of excellence' maps to 5.1 'Management commitment' and 5.3 'Quality policy' in ISO 9001.

How ISO 9001 and the EFQM Excellence Model compare				
EFQM Excellence Model criteria	**ISO 9001 requirements[1]**			
	Management responsibility	**Resource management**	**Product realization[2]**	**Measurement, analysis and improvement**
Leadership	✓			
Policy and strategy	✓		✓	✓
People	✓	✓		
Partnerships and resources		✓	✓	
Processes	✓	✓	✓	✓
Customer results	✓			✓
People results				
Society results				
Key performance results	✓		✓	✓

Note 1 Only the main linkages are shown.

Note 2 Product realization may be taken to include process management.

Example: Linking the Baldrige model and ISO 9001

If a business wanted to make a submission to the Malcolm Baldrige Award, when addressing Baldrige category 3 'Customer and Market Focus', it could also refer to the section in the ISO 9001 quality manual, 5.2 'Customer focus'.

These examples demonstrate how ISO 9001 provides support for the well-known quality models and that it has a consistent approach. The tables take this a stage further by defining the linkages between the different frameworks.

How ISO 9001 and the Baldrige model compare				
Baldrige Model criteria	**ISO 9001 requirements[1]**			
	Management responsibility	**Resource management**	**Product realization[2]**	**Measurement, analysis and improvement**
Leadership	✓			✓
Strategic planning	✓	✓		✓
Customer and market focus	✓		✓	✓
Information and analysis			✓	✓
Human resource focus	✓	✓		
Process management	✓		✓	✓
Business results	✓	✓	✓	✓

Note 1 Only the main linkages are shown.

Note 2 Product realization may be taken to include process management.

Part 2: ISO 9001 and the business improvement approaches

Introduction

The business improvement approaches described can be used to support ISO 9001 and other business improvement models. This section provides:

- a thumbnail description of all the business improvement approaches included;
- a summary table, outlining the factors to consider for the use of each approach;
- an explanation of each business improvement approach.

Each business improvement approach is explained using a common format:

- brief background;
- basic principles;
- description;
- a table giving guidance on how the approach is best used.

The following table lists the factors that will guide your choice of a particular approach.

Factor	Description	Options
Link to main ISO 9001 requirements	Where the approach supports ISO 9001	Management responsibility **(MR)**, Resource management **(RM)**, Process management **(PR)**, Measurement and analysis **(M&A)**, Improvement **(Imp)**
Scope of use	Type of organization	Private, public/voluntary, SME
	Where the approach was designed for use	UK, Europe, USA, global
	Industry	Manufacturing or service
	Where the approach may be used	Function, division and/or organization
Degree of change in systems	How much change to the systems and approaches will be encountered day to day within the organization	Large, medium, small
Degree of change for people	How much people will be affected by the change	Large, medium, small

Introduction

Factor	Description	Options
Level of benefit	How much benefit will be derived from the change	Large, medium, small
Level of involvement	How people will be involved in the change	Fully inclusive, inclusive, coercive
Maturity level	Who should use the approach	Beginner, experienced, world-class
Timescale	How long it will take to implement the approach	Less than 3 months, 6–12 months, over 12 months
Level of investment	What it will cost in terms of resource and expenditure	High, medium, low
How to implement	How to get started	Evolution, project or programme

The business improvement approaches

Quality approach	Thumbnail description
Balanced Scorecards (BSC)	A framework for defining performance measures.
Benchmarking	Measurement and process improvement based on investigating the approaches taken by other organizations.
Best Value	Seeks to improve local government performance in service delivery by ensuring that the cost and quality of the services are at a level acceptable to local customers.
Better Quality Service Reviews (BQSR)	Management driving forward continuous service improvement based on improvement criteria and the selection of options.
Business Performance Improvement Review (BPIR)	Provides a framework that identifies how an organization prioritizes and responds to the needs of stakeholders.
Business Process Re-engineering (BPR)	Radically simplifying and eliminating processes throughout an organization to increase productivity and reduce cost.
Charter Mark	A scheme for encouraging and rewarding improvement in public service, similar approach to award submissions.
Failure Mode Effect Analysis (FMEA)	A tool for facilitating the process of predicting failures, planning preventive measures, estimating the cost of the failure, and planning redundant systems or system responses to failures.
Investors in People (IiP)	Effective investment in the training and development of people to achieve organizational goals.

Quality approach	Thumbnail description
Kaizen/Continuous Improvement	Incremental quality improvements through the involvement of people.
Kaizen Teams	Short duration improvement events that deliver major benefits with minimal investment.
Lean Thinking	Providing a way to do more with less: less human effort, less equipment, less time and less space.
Performance Measurement	The identification of areas for improvement by measuring current performance and comparing against desired performance.
Process Classification Framework (PCF)	A list of common processes that aids process identification and benchmarking activities.
Process Management	Improvement through understanding the key business processes which are most in need of improvement.
Self-assessment	Reviewing the results, approaches and their deployment using a Quality Model (eg, the EFQM Excellence Model).
Six Sigma	Compares process performance against performance capability and empowers people to improve.
Statistical Process Control (SPC)	Reduction in waste and improvement in consistency through the reduction in variation.
Theory of Constraints	A systems approach to quality improvement that identifies and removes 'bottlenecks' in the system.
Total Productive Maintenance	Using a shop-floor approach to build an organization that prevents different types of losses (by ensuring zero accidents, zero defects, and zero failures) for the life of the production system.
Total Quality Management	A managed programme for improving all aspects of an organization through the involvement of its people.

How to use the business improvement approaches: summary tables

Pages 22–26 contain tables outlining the factors to consider for the use of each business improvement approach. The tables are followed by more detailed information on the approaches.

Approach	Balanced Scorecards	Benchmarking	Best Value	Better Quality Service Reviews

Link to ISO 9001	✓ MR
	  RM
	✓ PR
	✓ M&A
	✓ Imp
		MR
		RM
		PR
		M&A
		✓ Imp
			✓ MR
			  RM
			✓ PR
			✓ M&A
			  Imp
				✓ MR
				  RM
				✓ PR
				✓ M&A
				✓ Imp

Scope of use	Function, division and/or organization	Function	Function and organization	Function/service
Degree of change in systems	Large if no measurement is in place already	Large to medium	Medium	Large to medium
Degree of change to people	Large if no measurement is in place already. The change in approach to measurement is likely to change people's behaviour	Large to medium	Medium	Large to medium depending on option selected
Level of benefit	Medium	Large	Medium	Depends on the base-line performance
Level of involvement	Usually inclusive if scorecards are widely deployed	Inclusive	Inclusive	Often coercive
Maturity level	Any	Experienced and world-class	Beginner	Any
Timescale	Less than 3 months, but could be longer if there is no existing measurement	6–12 months	6–12 months	Over 12 months
Level of investment	Low	High	Medium	Medium
How to implement	Project	Project	Project	Programme for all services

Approach	Business Performance Improvement Review	Business Process Re-engineering	Charter Mark	Failure Mode Effect Analysis
Link to ISO 9001	✓ MR ✓ RM ✓ PR ✓ M&A ✓ Imp	MR RM PR M&A ✓ Imp	MR ✓ RM ✓ PR ✓ M&A ✓ Imp	MR RM ✓ PR ✓ M&A ✓ Imp
Scope of use	Division or organization	Division or organization	Division or organization	Mainly manufacturing/ product or service
Degree of change in systems	Medium	Large	Small	Small
Degree of change to people	Medium	Large	Small	Small
Level of benefit	Medium	Large	Small	Large
Level of involvement	Fully inclusive	Often coercive	Fully inclusive	Fully inclusive
Maturity level	Beginner, experienced and world-class	Any	Beginner	Experienced
Timescale	6–12 months	6–12 months	6–12 months	6–12 months
Level of investment	Medium	High	Low	Low
How to implement	Project	Project	Project	Project

Approach	Investors in People	Kaizen/ Continuous Improvement	Kaizen Teams	Lean Thinking
Link to ISO 9001	✓ MR ✓ RM PR ✓ M&A ✓ Imp	MR ✓ RM ✓ PR M&A ✓ Imp	MR ✓ RM ✓ PR M&A ✓ Imp	MR RM ✓ PR ✓ M&A ✓ Imp
Scope of use	Organization	Division or organization	Contained functional unit	Organization
Degree of change in systems	Medium	Small	Medium	Large
Degree of change to people	Large	Large	Small	Large
Level of benefit	Medium	Large to medium depending on the success of implementation	Large	Large
Level of involvement	Fully inclusive	Fully inclusive	Fully inclusive	Coercive
Maturity level	Beginner	Beginner	Experienced or world-class	Experienced or world-class
Timescale	Depends on commitment. Typically 6 months to 2 years	Over 12 months	Less than 3 months	Over 12 months
Level of investment	Low	High	Low	Medium
How to implement	Programme	Programme	Project	Programme

Approach	Performance Measurement	Process Classification Framework	Process Management	Self-assessment
Link to ISO 9001	✓ MR RM ✓ PR ✓ M&A ✓ Imp	MR RM ✓ PR M&A Imp	✓ MR ✓ RM ✓ PR ✓ M&A ✓ Imp	✓ MR RM PR ✓ M&A ✓ Imp
Scope of use	Function, division or organization	Function, division or organization	Function	Function, division or organization
Degree of change in systems	Small	Not applicable	Varies, depending on degree of change required	Small
Degree of change to people	Medium	Not applicable	Varies, depending on degree of change required	Small
Level of benefit	Medium	Medium	Varies, depending on degree of change required	Medium
Level of involvement	Inclusive	Inclusive	Inclusive	Inclusive
Maturity level	All	Beginner	All	All – but the approach used will vary
Timescale	Less than 3 months	Less than 3 months	Over 12 months	Depends on approach; less than 3 months or 6–12 months
Level of investment	Low	Low	Depends on improvement method used	Medium to low
How to implement	Project	Project	Evolution or project	Project

Approach	Six Sigma	Statistical Process Control	Theory of Constraints	Total Productive Maintenance	Total Quality Management
Link to ISO 9001	✓ MR ✓ RM ✓ PR ✓ M&A ✓ Imp	MR RM PR ✓ M&A Imp	MR ✓ RM ✓ PR M&A ✓ Imp	MR ✓ RM ✓ PR ✓ M&A ✓ Imp	✓ MR ✓ RM ✓ PR ✓ M&A ✓ Imp
Scope of use	Organization	Organization	Function	Function	Division or organization
Degree of change in systems	Medium	Medium	Medium to small	Small	Small
Degree of change to people	Medium	Medium	Medium	Large	Large
Level of benefit	Large	Large	Medium	Large to medium depending on the success of implement-ation	Large to medium depending on the success of implement-ation
Level of involvement	Fully inclusive	Fully inclusive	Inclusive	Fully inclusive	Fully inclusive
Maturity level	All levels	All levels	Experienced or world-class	All levels	Beginner
Timescale	Over 12 months	Over 12 months	Over 12 months	Over 12 months	Over 12 months
Level of investment	High, due to training costs	Medium, due to training costs	Low to medium	Medium	High
How to implement	Programme	Programme	Evolution	Programme	Programme

Balanced Scorecard

How to use

Factor	Comments				
Link to ISO 9001	MR	RM	PR	M&A	Imp
	✓		✓	✓	✓
Scope of use	All types of organization Both manufacturing and service Function, division and/or organization				
Degree of change in systems	Large if no measurement is in place already				
Degree of change to people	Large if no measurement is in place already. The change in approach to measurement is likely to change people's behaviour				
Level of benefit	Medium				
Level of involvement	Usually inclusive if scorecards are widely deployed				
Maturity level	Any				
Timescale	Less than 3 months, but could be longer if there is no existing measurement				
Level of investment	Low				
How to implement	Project				

Background

This approach has its origins in a one-year research project conducted in 1990 that examined performance measurement in the future. The concern at the time was that performance measurement was essentially financial and that this was hindering organizations' ability to create future economic value.

David Norton, the CEO of Nolan Norton, served as the study leader and Robert Kaplan as the academic consultant. The research study considered innovative performance measurement systems and this led to the publication of a *Harvard Business Review* article in January-February 1992 entitled 'The Balanced Scorecard. Measures that Drive Performance' Their book, *The Balanced Scorecard*, followed this article in 1996. More recently, Kaplan and Norton's book *The Strategy Focused Organization* (2001) reinforced the use of the Balanced Scorecard to deliver organizational strategy.

It is important to note that although the Balanced Scorecard was developed based on the observation of private organizations, the principles are equally applicable to public and voluntary organizations. A number of examples are available to reinforce this point.

Principles

The main principle behind the Balanced Scorecard is that traditional financial measures, which tell the story of past events, are now inadequate. In the industrial age, long-term capabilities and customer relationships were not critical for success. In the information age, there is a need for measures that guide and evaluate an organization's journey to create future value through investment in customers, suppliers, employees, processes, technology and innovation.

The Balanced Scorecard couples the financial measures of past performance with measures of the drivers of future performance. This leads to four perspectives:

1. Financial perspective: how is the organization doing financially?
2. Customer perspective: who are our customers and what do they think of us?
3. Internal/business-process perspective: how good are we at delivering customer satisfaction and achieving the financial objectives?
4. Learning and growth perspective: what capabilities must we develop longer-term?

The concept of 'balance' comes from the need to have representative measures from each perspective, recognizing that the perspectives are also linked:

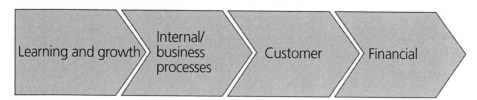

Approach

The starting point for the development of a Balanced Scorecard is referral to the organization's vision and strategy. Once this has been established four questions should be posed, one for each perspective:

1. Financial: to succeed financially, how should we appear to our shareholders?
2. Customer: to achieve our vision, how should we appear to our customers?
3. Internal/business processes: to satisfy our shareholders and customers, which business processes must we excel at?
4. Learning and growth: to achieve our vision, how will we sustain our ability to change and improve? (Source: Kaplan and Norton, 1996)

It is normal to identify a number of potential measures for the scorecard. The key to the effective use of the approach is to ensure that the measures finally chosen relate to the achievement of the vision and strategy, and that they maintain the 'balance' by including all perspectives.

Several factors are recorded for each measure selected:

- the specific objective;
- definition of the measure,
- target;
- any related initiatives supporting the delivery of the target.

It is also common for scorecards to be cascaded through an organization, with a corporate scorecard supported by divisional scorecards, which in turn are supported by unit scorecards.

Benchmarking

How to use

Benchmarking can take many forms depending on the scope of the study. The following table gives a view of a general best practice study.

Factor	Comments				
Link to ISO 9001	MR	RM	PR	M&A	Imp ✓
Scope of use	All types of organization Both manufacturing and service Functional				
Degree of change in systems	Large to medium				
Degree of change to people	Large to medium				
Level of benefit	Large				
Level of involvement	Inclusive				
Maturity level	Experienced and world-class				
Timescale	6–12 months				
Level of investment	High				
How to implement	Project				

Background

Benchmarking has become a common term since it was popularized by Xerox in the 1980s. There is a distinction between the word 'benchmark' and the process of 'benchmarking'. In terms of quality improvement, a benchmark is a 'best-in-class' achievement. This achievement then becomes the reference point or recognized standard of excellence against which similar processes are measured.

While a benchmark is a measure, 'benchmarking' is a process of measurement that can contribute to achieving competitive advantage:

'Benchmarking is the process of continuously comparing and measuring an organization with business leaders anywhere in the world to gain information which will help the organization take action to improve its performance.' (Tanner and Walker, 2003)

There are two distinct approaches to benchmarking: competitive benchmarking and process benchmarking.

Competitive benchmarking measures organizational performance against that of competing organizations. It tends to concentrate on the relative performance of competitors using a select set of measures.

Process benchmarking measures discrete process performance and functionality against organizations that lead in those processes. It seeks the best practice for conducting a particular business process after first validating that the performance of that process is world class. Once the best practice is identified and understood, it may then be adapted and improved for application to another organization.

There are several types of benchmarking, ranging from internal benchmarking to worldwide best practice benchmarking. As a general observation, the wider the scope of the study the longer it takes to complete, the more money it costs, but the greater the level of benefit.

Benchmarking can be highly effective for improving performance. It can be used either as a tool in itself, or as an element of a Business Process Re-engineering project. In either case it:

- develops realistic stretch goals;
- establishes realistic action plans;
- encourages a striving for excellence and innovation;
- creates a better understanding of your current position;
- underpins the drive for performance improvement.

Principles

Benchmarking aims to provide goals for realistic process improvement and an understanding of the changes necessary to facilitate that improvement. It contains a bias for action that can lead to breakthrough and continuous improvement projects for products, services or processes. The results of benchmarking should be increased customer satisfaction and improved competitive position.

Approach

Benchmarking studies generally follow a four-step process:

1. Planning a benchmarking project.
2. Collecting data.
3. Analysing the data for performance gaps and process enablers.
4. Improving by adapting process enablers.

Benchmarking

The Benchmarking 'roadmap' shows that there are a number of stakeholders involved in the approach.

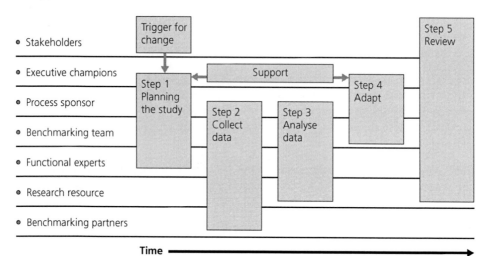

source: Tanner and Walker 2003

The first step of the approach is to plan for the study, as benchmarking is a project-based approach. This step includes the need to better understand the organization and the area to be benchmarked.

Data collection for benchmarking studies can take many forms: telephone surveys, written questionnaires, literature searches, exchange of prepared materials, or site visits.

A benchmarking study will provide outputs. It should:

- provide a measure that compares performance for the benchmarked process among the target organizations;
- describe the organization's gap in performance as compared to these identified performance levels;
- identify best practices and enablers that produced these results observed during the study;
- set performance goals for the process and identify areas where action can be taken to improve the sponsoring organization's performance. The sponsoring organization is then responsible for implementing the action plan.

Best Value

How to use

Factor	Comments				
Link to ISO 9001	MR ✓	RM	PR ✓	M&A ✓	Imp
Scope of use	Public sector organizations Service Function and organization				
Degree of change in systems	Medium				
Degree of change to people	Medium				
Level of benefit	Medium				
Level of involvement	Inclusive				
Maturity level	Beginner				
Timescale	6–12 months				
Level of investment	Medium				
How to implement	Project				

Background

Best Value was introduced as a local government policy in 1997, after the election of a Labour administration in the United Kingdom. The policy was designed to reconfigure service delivery by local government, with local authorities assuming the role of enabling organizations rather than service providers.

Local authorities are examining the way that they work, including organizational structure and internal management information requirements. Best Value has coincided with a number of other local government reforms which are emphasizing strategic decision-making; accountability; transparency; sound governance and an awareness of the citizen's perspective.

Principles

Best Value guidance suggests managers should set objectives and measures and then prioritize areas with the greatest scope for improvement. It recommends that priorities should be set using the following '4 Cs' principles:

1. Challenge: 'Why are we doing this?' The object should be to learn about the 'what' and 'why' of current performance.
2. Compare: Government promotes the concept of benchmarking.
3. Consult: Consulting with users and consumers to improve service.
4. Compete: The fourth 'C' replaces Compulsory Competitive Tendering (CCT).

Approach

Best Value follows an inclusive approach, involving working sessions to complete the work in a project-based fashion.

In a typical project, a first session focuses on the core concepts and includes discussions on organizational structure; strategic decision making; concepts of quality; benchmarking; reconfiguring service delivery options and the partnership approach. This first session uses brainstorming to crystallize a number of ideas:

- a recognition that the organization's structure needs to change;
- decisions are not being made with a strategic view in mind; instead committees tend to operate in an incremental fashion, without innovative thought;
- the lack of linkage between area committees and any form of decision-making with regard to budgetary or service delivery issues.

A second session focuses to a greater extent on the regulatory environment; the technicalities of activity-based costing; three-year budgeting; performance measurement systems and the individual circumstances of an organization.

The main function of the sessions is to establish a set of terms to try to change organizational culture. They provide a common set of values to facilitate better communication.

Better Quality Service Reviews (BQSR)

How to use

The Better Quality Service initiative is aimed at public sector organizations, but the principles are applicable to all organizations.

Factor	Comments				
Link to ISO 9001	MR ✓	RM	PR ✓	M&A ✓	Imp ✓
Scope of use	Public sector organizations Service Function/service				
Degree of change in systems	Large to medium				
Degree of change to people	Large to medium depending on option selected				
Level of benefit	Depends on the base-line performance				
Level of involvement	Often coercive				
Maturity level	Any				
Timescale	Over 12 months				
Level of investment	Medium				
How to implement	Programme for all services				

Background

Better Quality Service Reviews were developed to help central government organizations with the 'Modernizing Government' programme in the UK. They are a key part of their strategy to improve the level of service.

Published in 1998, the Government's handbook *Better Quality Services* sets out its desire to 're-invent Britain'. Part of this re-invention involves Government services delivering the highest quality, efficient, responsive and customer-focused services.

In the first phase of the programme, public sector organizations review their services and implement improvement actions based on these internal reviews. In the future, the Audit Commission will conduct independent audits to confirm that the best quality, most efficient service is being provided.

Principles

The Government has outlined a number of principles behind its Better Quality Services programme. These include:

- The Government is committed to value for money in public services.
- Better value for money and efficiency both mean better quality services for the customer at optimal cost to the taxpayer.
- Efficiency reviews should be regular, comprehensive and led and supported by senior managers.
- Full use should be made of Public Private Partnerships, using techniques, for example competition or benchmarking, which will produce best value for money in the particular circumstances.
- The scope for cross-departmental working, including through service level agreements, should be fully explored.

The decision on how to deliver best value for money should be based on a robust assessment of the options in each set of circumstances and must be publicly justifiable. There are a total of five options:

1. Abolish the service.
2. Restructure internally to improve the service.
3. Strategically contract-out the service if someone else can provide it better.
4. Market test to show that the department is best placed to deliver the service.
5. Privatize the service.

Other key points to remember are:

- Over a five-year period all of a department's services and activities should have been reviewed at least once.
- The search for improvement should be continuous.
- No services or activities should be excluded from reviews.
- No approach to improvement should be ruled out or accepted without a thorough examination of the options.

A typical approach has seven stages.

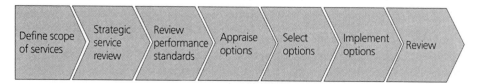

Define scope of services → Strategic service review → Review performance standards → Appraise options → Select options → Implement options → Review

The starting point is to define the scope of the service; this allows clarification and agreement on the service under review. Then the current and future needs of the service are determined along with the current performance. The review of current performance takes into account the Audit Commission's assessment methodology.

Once the required and actual levels of performance are known, each of the five Better Quality Service options can be appraised and the desired option selected and implemented.

Implementation may be achieved in-house, with the assistance of experienced change experts, or through a partnering approach. The final stage is a post-completion review of the activity so that continuous learning is possible.

Business Performance Improvement Review (BPIR)

How to use

Factor	Comments				
Link to ISO 9001	MR ✓	RM ✓	PR ✓	M&A ✓	Imp ✓
Scope of use	All types of organization, worldwide Both manufacturing and service Division and/or organization				
Degree of change in systems	Medium				
Degree of change to people	Medium				
Level of benefit	Medium				
Level of involvement	Fully inclusive				
Maturity level	Beginner, experienced and world-class				
Timescale	6–12 months				
Level of investment	Medium				
How to implement	Project				

Background

The Business Performance Improvement Review is based on the principles of ISO 9004:2000, Guidelines for Performance Improvement. The assessment element of BPIR is a unique offering of BSI Management Systems.

BPIR provides a framework that identifies how an organization prioritizes and responds to the needs of stakeholders through organizational policies, strategy and objectives.

The organization is able to prioritize the varying demands by implementing improvement initiatives through a clear understanding of:

- who the organization's stakeholders are, and
- the needs and expectations of the various stakeholders.

The benefits of implementing BPIR include:

- focus on business performance improvement opportunities;
- a balanced approach to business improvement;
- monitor and prioritize the needs of its stakeholders;
- focus on the necessary resources required to improve;
- improve existing business management systems.

Principles

BPIR aims to assess the extent to which an organization goes beyond the requirements of ISO 9001:2000 and incorporates principles based on ISO 9004:2000. It uses this information to focus on specific business needs – not just customer but also stakeholder needs.

ISO 9001:2000 is about customer focus. It is about turning customer requirements into customer satisfaction through the application of a management system.

ISO 9001:2000 Customer Requirements and Expectations

Focuses on the needs of the customer

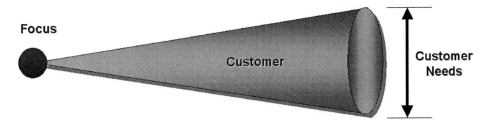

Nevertheless, much wider aspects affect an organization in addition to customers. These are the 'stakeholders' and include:

- customers;
- people in the organization;
- owners/shareholders;
- society;
- suppliers;
- any other stakeholders.

ISO 9004:2000 encourages the organization to look at all stakeholders.

ISO 9004:2000 Guidelines for Performance Improvements

All stakeholder needs

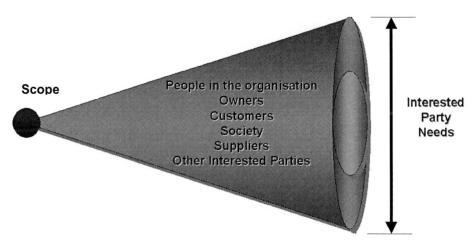

However, to try to manage all stakeholder needs all of the time is not always possible or acceptable. Therefore, a review using BPIR encourages organizations to prioritize their stakeholder needs in order to maximize benefits.

BSI Business Performance Improvement Review

Focus on appropriate stakeholder needs

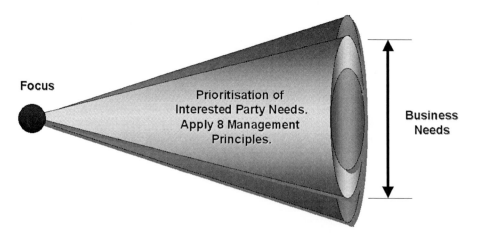

Approach

The review is performed in two phases. The first looks at the organization's strategic approach to stakeholders and management principles; the second verifies the organization's corresponding operational approach.

Review Process

The review will assess activities that contribute to performance improvement:

- the methods of identification and prioritization of the needs and expectations of stakeholders; and
- the effectiveness of the approaches designed to deliver upon the needs and expectations of stakeholders.

From the review, the organization is presented with a picture of the degree of effectiveness relating to the deployment and achievement of the various ongoing improvement initiatives.

This is then viewed against a balance between the various stakeholder needs and the management standard principles.

Business Process Re-engineering (BPR)

How to use

Factor	Comments				
Link to ISO 9001	MR	RM	PR	M&A	Imp ✓
Scope of use	All types of organization Both manufacturing and service Division or organization				
Degree of change in systems	Large				
Degree of change to people	Large				
Level of benefit	Large				
Level of involvement	Often coercive				
Maturity level	Any				
Timescale	6–12 months				
Level of investment	High				
How to implement	Project				

Background

Business process re-engineering was popularized in the early 1990s with publication of Hammer and Champy's best-selling book, *Reengineering the Corporation* (1993). The ideas built on the observation that organizations are sometimes faced with problems that need urgent attention. These could relate to survival, stakeholder pressure to change, or accelerated growth.

Such issues have to be tackled immediately, often with external help that brings expertise, resource and independence from the internal environment that may resist the change. Business Process Re-engineering, when used appropriately, may be used by any organization as the methodology to address the problems. With its focus on processes and consideration of people, it is an extremely powerful approach.

Business Process Re-engineering is often considered to be a cost-saving exercise. Intelligent re-engineering can also have a marked effect on customer satisfaction, operating flexibly and contributing significantly to the delivery of organizations' objectives. But above all, it solves the problems that initiated the project in the first place.

Principles

As defined by Hammer and Champy, re-engineering is:

'The fundamental rethinking and radical re-design of business processes to achieve dramatic improvements in critical, contemporary measures of performance, such as cost, quality, service and speed.'

This definition contains four key words:

1. *Fundamental:* Asking the most basic questions such as, 'Why do we want to do this?' and, 'Why do we want to do it in this way?'
2. *Radical:* By getting to the root of things. It is about reinvention not improvement.
3. *Dramatic:* Only to be used when a step change in performance is required.
4. *Processes:* Focusing on groups of activities and not individual tasks.

A study of organizations that have undertaken re-engineering highlights four common themes:

1. process orientation;
2. ambition;
3. rule-breaking;
4. creative use of information technology.

These themes underpin the re-engineering efforts.

Approach

Business process re-engineering is unique in that it is widely recognized that poor change management often leads to failure in delivery of the re-engineering project. In Hammer's later works, he admits that he had not put enough emphasis on the process focus.

There has also been wide debate on the right approach for Business Process Reengineering. This approach applies six steps to re-engineering and involves reviewing the current situation, developing a business model that addresses the issues at hand and planning implementation. Implementation itself is handled through the change management approach.

This approach combines the hard case for re-engineering with the softer 'people aspects', ensuring that the solution can be implemented with minimum problems. It uses a rigorous analytical method that takes into account the historical, political and cultural context of the work. By focusing on the few issues that cause the greatest number of problems, the approach produces rapid and focused results.

There is a strong emphasis on team working. Workshops are used to engage as many people as possible and to get buy-in to the changes. The ideas and output are verified throughout the project to ensure that the best solution is developed and that the project stays on track.

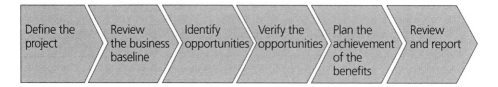

Define the project | Review the business baseline | Identify opportunities | Verify the opportunities | Plan the achievement of the benefits | Review and report

Step 1: Define the project

As with any major project the starting point is the project definition and the mobilization of the project team. One of the first tasks of the project team is to understand the context within which the re-engineering is to be delivered.

This is also the time to engage stakeholders by getting the scope of the work defined and authorized by the senior management team.

Step 2: Review the business baseline

It is important to develop hypotheses relating to the underlying cause of the problem at an early stage. Collect data to ascertain the current state of the area under review by carrying out 'business base-lining'. The key concept is to focus on 80 per cent of the costs so that time is not wasted searching for small gains.

Conduct process mapping to get a better understanding of the activities within the area. This leads to more detailed cost modelling and the identification of problems and needs.

Step 3: Identify opportunities

So far the activity has been reflective, revolving around the collection of data and formulation of ideas. Now start the process redesign and testing of the hypotheses developed in the previous stage.

A business model that captures the new way of working emerges. Where appropriate, apply investigative or even best practice benchmarking to develop the business model.

Step 4: Verify the opportunities

Test the derived solution against the problems to ensure that it solves them and meets the needs. At this stage the solution must be verified with the key stakeholders to make sure that it is acceptable.

Reviewing the solution against any benchmarking, if conducted, also provides a valuable test to ensure that the solution will be both effective and efficient.

Step 5: Plan the achievement of the benefits

Once the solution has been tested fully, start planning implementation. Implementation costs need to be identified, which may lead to a revision to the business model that has been developed.

As with any change programme there is likely to be resistance to change. This is only natural. A detailed understanding of both the costs and benefits allows the case for action to be made.

Step 6: Review and report

The final activity is a project report and a project review. This ensures that all the details of the project are recorded and that any learning is captured and shared.

Charter Mark

How to use

Charter Mark is only available for public sector organizations.

Factor	Comments				
Link to ISO 9001	MR	RM ✓	PR ✓	M&A ✓	Imp ✓
Scope of use	UK public sector organizations Sub-contractors providing public services Voluntary Division or organization				
Degree of change in systems	Small				
Degree of change to people	Small				
Level of benefit	Small				
Level of involvement	Fully inclusive				
Maturity level	Beginner				
Timescale	6–12 months				
Level of investment	Low				
How to implement	Project				

Background

Charter Mark is the government's 'customer service standard' for encouraging and rewarding improvement in public services. Applicants that are assessed as providing an excellent standard of service get the public recognition of the Charter Mark award. Charter Mark provides expert independent assessment and detailed feedback on how to improve, assisting organizations to meet public service delivery targets.

The benefits of gaining a Charter Mark include:

- A free audit with experienced assessors giving detailed feedback on the organization's performance. A recent study showed that 97 per cent of winners and 79 per cent of unsuccessful applicants had implemented assessors' feedback recommendations to some extent.
- Benchmarking – measured against the best public services.

- Recognition and positive publicity – national and local.
- Motivation and team building – rewards front-line staff and gives a big boost to morale.

Some 6,000 organizations have applied for Charter Mark and over 2,000 currently hold the award. The number of organizations applying has steadily increased.

Principles

Charter Mark focuses on the outcome for the customer while managing the needs of the community. It is flexible, easy to understand and applicable to all sizes of public sector organizations. Charter Mark is a standard of excellence, not a competition.

Approach

Organizations are assessed against six criteria:

1. **Set standards and perform well.** Show that your organization sets clear service and performance standards by consulting customers; meets those standards; monitors and reviews performance against standards and publishes results; and designs, puts into practice and monitors standards with as little unnecessary paperwork and administration as possible.
2. **Actively engage with your customers, partners and staff.** Show that your organization actively works with (engages with) customers, partners and staff to make sure it delivers high-quality services; consults and involves present and potential customers of public services, partners and staff; is open, and communicates clearly and effectively in plain language and in a number of different ways; and provides full information about services, their cost and how well they perform.
3. **Be fair and accessible to everyone and promote choice.** Show that your organization makes services easily available to everyone who needs them, offering choice wherever you can; and treats everybody fairly in access to services and service delivery, and pays particular attention to people with special needs.
4. **Continuously develop and improve.** Show that your organization always looks for ways to improve services and facilities, particularly when using technology; puts things right quickly and effectively; learns from, and improves as a result of, complaints, compliments and suggestions; and has a clear, well-publicized and easy-to-use complaints procedure, with the opportunity for independent review wherever possible.
5. **Use your resources effectively and imaginatively.** Show that your organization's financial management is effective; and you use resources effectively and imaginatively to provide best value for taxpayers and customers.
6. **Contribute to improving opportunities and quality of life in the communities you serve.** Show that your organization has reviewed and is aware of its impact and potential usefulness in the local and national communities you serve; and has made some

contribution to enriching the social or economic life of those communities, beyond the strict requirement of excellent service delivery, through positive, discretionary initiatives and imaginative use of resources.

Note: assessment and application methods may vary according to assessment body.

Organizations submit an application that is supported by evidence (no more than a box file). This is to show a high standard of service provision against each of the six criteria. Help is available to intending applicants in the form of a self-assessment toolkit and a programme of seminars where experienced assessors describe the evidence required and Charter Mark holders describe their experiences and give advice.

The length of time between deciding to apply for a Charter Mark Award and submitting the application will depend largely on the readiness of the organization. The self-assessment toolkit will assist in determining the organization's state of readiness and current level of performance against the six Charter Mark criteria. Once an organization considers that it has reached a satisfactory level of achievement against the requirements of the criteria, the production of an application and supporting evidence will depend on the size of the organization and the resources available to it. One local authority with substantial Charter Mark experience estimates that the average application will need 25 to 30 staff days for preparation.

After submitting an application, organizations receive a visit from an assessor who tests the evidence, follows up issues raised in the application and talks to customers, partners and staff involved with the service. A panel takes the final decision.

Applicants receive a feedback report from assessors identifying areas of weakness and making suggestions for improvement. Those not successful in winning an award can also attend a feedback meeting where they can discuss their application in more detail.

Failure Mode Effect Analysis (FMEA)

How to use

Factor	Comments				
Link to ISO 9001	MR	RM	PR ✓	M&A ✓	Imp ✓
Scope of use	Mainly manufacturing Product or service				
Degree of change in systems	Small				
Degree of change to people	Small				
Level of benefit	Large				
Level of involvement	Fully inclusive				
Maturity level	Experienced				
Timescale	6–12 months				
Level of investment	Low				
How to implement	Project				

Background

Failure Mode Effect Analysis was invented by NASA early in the US Apollo space programme. NASA created the tool to alleviate the stress between two conflicting mottos: 'Failure is not an option' and 'Perfect is the enemy of good'. The first meant successfully completing the mission and returning the crew. The second meant that failure of at least some components was unavoidable; the job was to predict them, prevent them when possible, plan for them, and build in the ability to overcome failures.

FMEA is a tool for facilitating the process of predicting failures, planning preventive measures, estimating the cost of the failure, and planning redundant systems or system responses to failures.

Principles

It is possible to analyse processes to determine possible modes of failure and their effects on the performance of the product or operation of the process or service system. FMEA is the study of potential failures to determine their effects. If the results of an FMEA are ranked in order of seriousness, this becomes Failure Mode Effect Criticality Analysis. The primary objective of an FMECA is to determine the features of process design or operation that are critical to the various modes of failure. It uses all the available experience and expertise, from marketing, design, technology, purchasing, production/operation, distribution, service, etc, to identify the importance levels or criticality of potential problems and stimulate action which will reduce these levels.

The elements of a complete FMECA are:

1. **Failure mode.** The anticipated conditions of operation are used as the background to study the most probable failure mode, location and mechanism of the process or system and its components.
2. **Failure effects.** The potential failures are studied to determine their probable effects on the performance of the whole process and the effects of the various components on each other.
3. **Failure criticality.** The potential failures in the various parts of the process or system are examined to determine the severity of each failure effect in terms of lowering of performance, safety hazard, total loss of function, etc.

FMECA may be applied at any stage of process design, development, or operation but since its main aim is to prevent failure, it is most suitably applied at the design stage to identify and eliminate causes. It may be appropriate to divide more complex processes or systems into sub-systems, each one being the subject of a separate FMECA.

Approach

Use this tool to:

- understand what can go wrong with a process or a product;
- understand how potential problems will affect customers' perceptions;
- provide suggestions for improvement when you plan to modify or introduce a new process or product. Be systematic in the analysis to make the best use of the tool.

When applying FMEA ensure there is a very thorough understanding of the product or process involved:

- have the product in front of you;
- visit the process;
- revisit the FMEA from time to time;
- review underlying assumptions against reality;
- revise and record any new assumptions.

FMECA pro formas are available which set out the steps of the analysis as follows:

1. Identify the process or system components, or process function.
2. List all possible failure modes of each component.

3. Set down the effects that each mode of failure would have on the overall function of the process or system.
4. List all the possible causes of each failure mode.
5. Assess the failure modes on a scale from 1 to 10. Experience and reliability data should be used, together with judgement, to determine the values for:

   P: the probability of each failure mode occurring (1 = low, 10 = high).

   S: the seriousness or criticality of the failure (1 = low, 10 = high).

   D: the difficulty of detecting the failure before the product or service is used by the consumer (1 = easy, 10 = very difficult).

Value	1	2	3	4	5	6	7	8	9	10
P	low chance of occurrence						almost certain to occur			
S	not serious, minor nuisance						total failure, safety hazard			
D	easily detected						unlikely to be detected			

Multiply the ratings together P x S x D = C. C is the criticality index or risk priority number (RPN) for each failure mode. This indicates the relative priority of each mode. When you have determined the value of C for each failure mode, rank the failures accordingly. In this way, the action required against each item can be judged in the light of the ranked severity and the resources available.

6. Indicate briefly on the pro forma the corrective action required and, if possible, which department or person is responsible and the expected completion date.

Example pro forma:

Step 1 Process Function	Step 2 Failure mode	Step 3 Effect	Step 4 Causes	Step 5 P	S	D	C	Step 6 Corrective action
Clarify request	Misunder-stand request	Wrong assessment of time required to repair. Late repair	Lack of inquiry	3	8	5	120	Develop inquiry guide with checklist
Take appoint-ment	Over-booking	Potential delays for customers	Planning not up to date	3	5	3	45	Automatic resource planning
etc								

Investors in People (IiP)

How to use

Factor	Comments				
Link to ISO 9001	MR ✓	RM ✓	PR	M&A ✓	Imp ✓
Scope of use	All types of organization Both manufacturing and service Organization				
Degree of change in systems	Medium				
Degree of change to people	Large				
Level of benefit	Medium				
Level of involvement	Fully inclusive				
Maturity level	Beginner				
Timescale	The length of time between making a commitment to achieve the standard and being recognized will vary from typically 6 months to 2 years, depending on the extent of development needed in the organization				
Level of investment	Low				
How to implement	Programme				

Background

Implemented in the early 1990s, Investors in People is a national standard that shows an organization has invested effectively in its employees and in doing so has improved its organizational effectiveness and service to the public.

The IiP initiative seeks to reward organizations that achieve the prescribed training and it allows them to display the IiP logo. The standard was based on UK organizations that had achieved a successful payback from investing in people. It has undergone some revisions since first being published. For example, a recent revision introduced two new areas:

'The organization is committed to ensuring equality of opportunity in the development of its people'.
'People believe their contribution to the organization is recognized'.

Principles

The Investors in People standard has four key principles:

1. **Commitment:** an Investor in People is fully committed to developing its people in order to achieve its organizational aims and objectives.
2. **Planning:** an Investor in People is clear about its aims and objectives and what its employees need to do to achieve them.
3. **Action:** an Investor in People develops its people effectively in order to improve its performance.
4. **Evaluation:** an Investor in People understands the impact of its investment in people on its performance.

An Investor in People recognizes employees as its most valuable asset and the development of employees is vital in order to improve service to the public. IiP is open to any organization of any size from any sector. Individual units of a larger organization may also apply.

Approach

Becoming an Investor in People involves a number of stages:

1. **Information gathering:** including finding out more about the standard and its application.
2. **Initial assessment** to see how the organization measures up against the national standard and identify action to close any gaps.
3. **Develop** people and processes as necessary.
4. **Further assessment:** once your organization meets the standard it will be formally recognized as an Investor in People and can publicize this through use of the logo.
5. **Re-assessment:** organizations will need to decide how often they wish to be reviewed against the standard. There is no minimum or recommended time period between post-recognition reviews, although the maximum is three years. The timing should ensure that continuous improvement becomes an integral part of retaining the standard.

During the assessment, assessors look for:

- effective service planning taking place, involving employees wherever possible;
- effective workforce planning taking place where key training and development issues that will help service delivery are identified at the corporate, directorate and service level;
- all employees getting an effective appraisal where training and development needs are identified in line with business needs;
- training and development, including induction and on-the-job development, taking place;
- all training and development activity being evaluated against its original objectives at the individual, team and organizational level.

When conducting the re-assessments, the assessors will check areas where improvement was shown to be necessary at the last assessment, such as:

- communication with employees, both individually and with teams;
- evaluation of training and development at all levels;
- service areas that were shown to be particularly weak at the last assessment;
- full involvement of 'fringe areas', geographical or otherwise;
- effective monitoring of processes, ie service planning, appraisal, induction, performance indicators.

The benefits of Investors in People for the organization are:

- a more systematic approach to training, a clearer focus on training based on business needs and better value from its training spend;
- improved employee communications and a better understanding of the business among employees;
- a higher level of motivation among the workforce;
- a more skilled workforce;
- increased profitability.

The benefits of Investors in People for the individual are:

- increased job satisfaction;
- the training and development to enable him or her to do a good job;
- recognition and structured development;
- a greater sense of pride in the organization;
- improved motivation and commitment.

Kaizen/Continuous Improvement

How to use

Factor	Comments				
Link to ISO 9001	MR	RM ✓	PR ✓	M&A	Imp ✓
Scope of use	All types of organization Both manufacturing and service Division or organization				
Degree of change in systems	Small				
Degree of change to people	Large				
Level of benefit	Large to medium depending on the success of implementation				
Level of involvement	Fully inclusive				
Maturity level	Beginner				
Timescale	Over 12 months				
Level of investment	High				
How to implement	Programme				

Background

Kaizen is the Japanese philosophy of continuous improvement, making simple, small, incremental improvements that are not costly but result in real cost savings, better quality and higher productivity.

Interest in Japanese approaches increased in the 1960s and 1970s, when Western organizations faced new competition from a part of the world that had previously been known for producing shoddy, cheap goods. Here was a new competitor that was not only lower priced, but also produced goods of higher quality and specification. The 'revolution' had been led by two Americans, Dr Deming and Dr Juran, who at the time received no airtime for their ideas in their country of origin.

Principles

The main principle behind Kaizen is embedded in the Deming Cycle.

source: Deming 1994

There are many other principles that support the Plan – Do – Check – Act element of continuous improvement: management, 'process vs results', putting quality first and 'the next process is the customer'.

Management

The Japanese believe this comprises two major functions: maintenance and improvement. *Maintenance* refers to activities directed toward maintaining current technological, managerial, and operating standards and upholding such standards through training and discipline. Under its maintenance function, management performs its assigned tasks so that everybody can follow standard operating procedures (SOPs). *Improvement* refers to activities directed toward raising current standards.

It is suggested that because of their fascination with innovation, Western managers tend to be impatient and overlook the long-term benefits Kaizen can bring to an organization. Kaizen emphasizes human efforts, morale, communication, training, teamwork, involvement, and self-discipline – a commonsense, low-cost approach to improvement.

'Process vs results'

Kaizen fosters process-oriented thinking, since processes must be improved for results to improve. Failure to achieve planned results indicates a failure in the process. Management must identify and correct such process-based errors. Kaizen focuses on human efforts – an orientation that contrasts sharply with the results-based thinking of the West.

Putting quality first

Of the primary goals of quality, cost and delivery, quality should always have the highest priority. No matter how attractive the price and delivery terms offered to the customer, the company would not be able to compete if the product or service lacked quality. Practising a quality-first credo requires management commitment because managers often face the temptation to make compromises to meet delivery requirements or cut costs. In doing so, they risk sacrificing not only quality but the life of the business as well.

Kaizen is a problem-solving process. In order for a problem to be correctly understood and solved, it must be recognized and the relevant data gathered and analysed. Trying to solve a problem without hard data is not scientific or objective. Collecting data on the current status focuses activity and serves as a starting point for improvement.

Once a problem has been identified and corrective action taken, action should be taken to prevent a recurrence. This activity is termed 'mistake proofing' or *Poke Yoke* in Japanese. Take an example where a part can be put onto an assembly in one of two ways – the right way or the wrong way. Mistake proofing would involve changing the assembly so that it was only possible to fit the part in the right way.

The next process is the customer

All work is a series of processes, and each process has its supplier as well as its customer. A material or a piece of information provided by process A (supplier) is worked on and improved in process B and then sent on to process C. The next process should always be regarded as a customer. This applies to two types of customers: internal (within the company) and external (out in the market).

Most people working in an organization deal with internal customers. This realization should lead to a commitment never to pass on defective parts or inaccurate pieces of information to those in the next process. When everybody in the organization practises this, the external customer receives a high-quality product or service as a result.

Approach

There are many approaches to implementing Kaizen each with their individual features. These approaches have several things in common:

- the need to gain management commitment;
- educating all staff in the need for customer focus and for the reduction in process variation;
- process-oriented management;
- problem solving including the use of the seven quality tools.

The seven quality tools are:

1. Pareto diagrams.
2. Cause and effect/fishbone diagrams.
3. Histograms.
4. Control charts.
5. Scatter diagrams.
6. Graphs.
7. Check sheets/tally charts.

In latter years the Kaizen principles were extended to develop 'Total Quality Management' programmes (see 'Total Quality Management (TQM)' on page 93 for more information).

Kaizen Teams

How to use

Factor	Comments				
Link to ISO 9001	MR	RM ✓	PR ✓	M&A	Imp ✓
Scope of use	All types of organization Both manufacturing and service, but most success has been with manufacturing units Contained functional unit				
Degree of change in systems	Medium				
Degree of change to people	Small				
Level of benefit	Large				
Level of involvement	Fully inclusive				
Maturity level	Experienced or world-class				
Timescale	Less than 3 months				
Level of investment	Low				
How to implement	Project				

Background

Kaizen, or continuous improvement, has helped many organizations improve their performance by changing the culture of the organization. A Kaizen organization will have effective communication, widespread teamwork, a focus on facts and processes, and will be seeking to move forward a little bit every day.

The idea of Kaizen teams has become very popular on the back of the other Japanese approaches, such as just-in-time and lean engineering. The approach described here was developed by the Association of Manufacturing Excellence (AME) and is called 'The Kaizen Blitz'.

Benefits of this approach can include:

* 90 per cent reductions in set up time in 1 week;
* 20–60 per cent improvements in productivity in 4 days;
* inventories cut in half in only a few days;

- process time reductions of 40–80 per cent;
- walking distance reductions of 40–90 per cent.

Principles

- Kaizen Blitz is doing, not proposing. This is different from traditional Kaizen approaches such as Quality Circles.
- Getting dirty together. It is a hands-on process where every team member gets involved.
- Kaizen Blitz is a low-budget process. A typical budget would be $300–400. There is no time to get capital equipment in the five days it takes to run the project.
- In the long run, only the simple things work. Complex solutions are hard to maintain and harder to monitor.

During a Kaizen Blitz project there are a number of rules:

- Be open-minded.
- Maintain a positive attitude.
- Reject excuses – seek solutions.
- Ask Why?, Why? – there are no stupid questions.
- Take action – don't seek perfection, implement now with the resources at hand.
- Use all the team's knowledge.
- Disregard rank – everyone is equal.
- Just do it!

Approach

Kaizen Blitz builds on other programmes such as TQM and world-class manufacturing. It is a natural next step once the basics of continuous improvement are in place and there is a need for a step change in performance. The approach is also highly focused. The step change is made in a limited scope area (a work location or cell – not a factory).

In a typical project, a cross-functional, multi-level team of 6–12 members work for 12–14 hours a day for 3–4 days. They rapidly develop, test and refine solutions to problems and leave a new process in place. A key feature is they don't plan, they don't propose, they do.

Kaizen Blitzing is a top-down process beginning with the process owner. The process owner could be at any level, but he or she will be in charge. It is a team process with core staff from the area being tackled making up the team. The team is brought together at the start of the project and educated in the concepts and tools. Kaizen experts do the training and facilitate the process.

Lean Thinking

How to use

Factor	Comments				
Link to ISO 9001	MR	RM	PR ✓	M&A ✓	Imp ✓
Scope of use	All types of organization Both manufacturing and service, but most success has been with manufacturing units Organization				
Degree of change in systems	Large				
Degree of change to people	Large				
Level of benefit	Large				
Level of involvement	Coercive				
Maturity level	Experienced or world-class				
Timescale	Over 12 months				
Level of investment	Medium				
How to implement	Programme				

Background

In *The Machine that Changed the World* (1991) a wealth of benchmarking data shows that there is a better way to organize and manage customer relations. The study focused mainly on the practices from Japan, and notably the Toyota Production System.

A follow-up work, *Lean Thinking* (1996), sought to explain the approaches that led to the results. The practices have now spread to Europe and into service industries.

Lean Thinking has its roots in 'Systems thinking'. Systems thinking recognizes that simple, logical, step-by-step approaches are an over-simplification of the real world. In reality, even a simple process is contained within a system and the parts of the system will affect the operation of the system.

Take filling a bath as an example of systems thinking. You turn the tap and water flows from it. This causes an increase in the water level in the bath and as the water reaches the desired level the tap is turned to reduce the flow, to the point when no more water flows from it. This is a simple system.

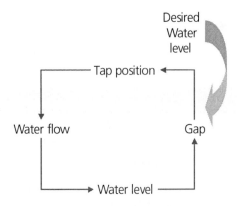

source: Senge 1993

Principles

A key concept is the reduction of waste; there are five principles:

1. **Specify value.** First there is a need to define exactly what is meant by value – this is what the customer actually wants (but they may not be expressing this clearly). Value also needs to be defined in terms of the whole product, not just part of it.
2. **Identify the value stream** – the path that the product or service takes.
3. **Flow** – converting from the world of batch and queue is one of the most difficult barriers to overcome.
4. **Pull.** Nothing is produced up stream until a down stream customer asks for it. The key to pull is having a responsive system and not having stocks. The need to prepare for pull also has an effect on how you organize.
5. **Perfection** is all about getting things right first time. Kaizen workshops are held regularly to improve the business. Typically these last 2–3 days. This does not rule out a radical path to perfection. This is achieved, for example, by reconfiguring the value stream.

The principles build on the idea of Just-in-Time (JiT) manufacturing. Parts are delivered not only at the right time and in the right quantity, but are synchronized to the customer's schedules so that they match the customer's own product flow, completely eliminating stock held next to the assembly track. A common example is in the manufacture of car seats. As they take up so much space they cannot be stored in the assembly area, and because they vary in colour and trim material from one vehicle to the next, they need to be delivered in sequence according to the specification of cars passing down the track – typically from a nearby supplier park.

Just-in-Sequence delivery requires effective systems for sharing information between customer and supplier and a high degree of integration between the two operations. The next step is for supplier personnel to be responsible for final assembly on the track – still an unusual arrangement.

Approach

Step 1: find a change agent and educate the people who will be involved in the project

It is useful to find a reason for starting the change by seizing a crisis or by creating one, because the principles of Lean Thinking require people to go against their natural instincts. For example, logic dictates that keeping a stock of finished goods is the only way to protect supply and deliver customer service. In Lean Thinking people have to accept that zero stock is the way forward and will be something new.

Lean principles should be introduced in a controlled and systematic way. The advice is to concentrate on getting the principles introduced in a small way before focusing on the wider strategy.

Step 2: map the value streams

Start by mapping the value streams of one important and visible activity. Then the changes needed can be identified. Make the changes and check the results; only if this is successful should the scope of the programme be expanded.

Step 3: change the organization

Change the organization to support the value streams. Some organizations reorganize themselves by product family and value stream to achieve this rather than by function. As there will be a high level of change, a lean promotion function may be created to give the programme focus and support. This can be part of the growth strategy.

As people will be affected by the change, dealing with excess people at the outset of the programme will be key to the programme success. It is also important to remove those who attempt to slow down the programme.

The approach is considered to be a programme and not a project, as improvements are always being sought. The advice is that 'When you have fixed something, fix it again'. It is also acceptable to take two steps forward and one step back, but 'No steps forward is not ok'.

Performance Measurement

How to use

Factor	Comments				
Link to ISO 9001	MR ✓	RM	PR ✓	M&A ✓	Imp ✓
Scope of use	All types of organization Both manufacturing and service Function, division or organization				
Degree of change in systems	Small				
Degree of change to people	Medium				
Level of benefit	Medium				
Level of involvement	Inclusive				
Maturity level	Beginner, experienced and world-class				
Timescale	Less than 3 months				
Level of investment	Low				
How to implement	Project				

Background

It is often said that it is impossible to manage what cannot be measured. And organizations often have very poor performance measurement systems.

A Performance Management Framework (PMF) is a mechanism for managing an organization through the identification of a number of critical measures and monitoring the current and planned performance.

Based on a balanced scorecard approach, the measures are developed from the organization's Mission and Critical Success Factors. The approach is of benefit to all organizations and has been used successfully in both private and public organizations of varying sizes.

The main benefits are:

- The approach links strategy with action and gives a simple view of performance status. The management summary may be understood at a glance.

- All stakeholder interests are represented and minimal effort is needed to collect performance data.
- The design of the PMF allows easy access to detail as needed as the performance is reviewed.
- Management decisions are made with more confidence and debates are fact-based as opposed to being fact-free.

Principles

Traditionally performance measures and indicators have been derived from financial information, which measures how successful or not the organization has been in the past, but says nothing about current or future performance.

Kaplan and Norton first introduced the balanced scorecard concept in 1992. It views an organization from four vital perspectives:

- financial (past);
- process (current);
- customer (current);
- learning and growth (future).

There are also two fundamental performance measurement types:

- **Outcome measures** (sometimes known as 'lag indicators') which show the performance of an organization against *what* it must achieve to meet its mission, where the organization wants to be *in the future*.
- **Driver measures** (sometimes known as 'lead indicators') which show the performance of the organization's processes, *how* the outcomes will be achieved, how the organization is performing *now*.

Poor performance of the drivers will lead to the outcomes not being achieved, so the business will fail to meet its objectives or mission.

Approach

The approach follows a five-stage 'DRIVE' sequence:

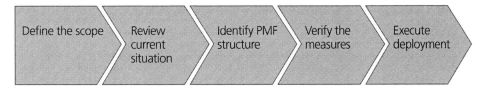

Define the scope → Review current situation → Identify PMF structure → Verify the measures → Execute deployment

Define the scope

As with any major project the starting point is the project definition and the mobilization of the project team. This is also the time to engage stakeholders by getting the scope of the work defined and authorized by the senior management team.

Review the current situation

Identify the current Critical Success Factors (CSFs), Key Performance Indicators (KPIs) and other available measures. Ownership of the measures must be considered at this stage to prevent issues later on in the work.

Identify the PMF structure

Identify potential measures. These will be at both the strategic (CSF) and operational (KPI) levels. Targets, the potential data collection system, measurement medium, measurement structure and responsibilities all have to be agreed.

Verify the measures

Check that the measures are balanced before they are verified with the key stakeholders and the organization. Part of this stage includes performing 'dry runs' to ensure that the resulting system will meet the organization's needs.

Execute deployment

Develop an implementation plan, with targets for putting each measure in place to establish regular data collection and usage. It is normal to produce a review schedule against which implementation is monitored. This schedule evolves into an ongoing systematic review of the PMF – are the measures beneficial, relevant and being used to manage the business?

Other considerations

The PMF approach is most effective once an organization has come to terms with its direction and critical success factors. For organizations that have not reached this point, it might be appropriate to start with Direction Setting and Visioning activity. Alternatively a Performance Management System may already be in place.

Process Classification Framework (PCF)

How to use

The Process Classification Framework is a universal tool. It is particularly useful for newcomers to process management.

Factor	Comments				
Link to ISO 9001	MR	RM	PR ✓	M&A	Imp
Scope of use	All types of organization Both manufacturing and service Function, division or organization				
Degree of change in systems	Not applicable				
Degree of change to people	Not applicable				
Level of benefit	Medium				
Level of involvement	Inclusive				
Maturity level	Beginner				
Timescale	Less than 3 months				
Level of investment	Low				
How to implement	Project				

Background

The American Productivity and Quality Center (APQC) was founded in 1977 as a non-profit organization working with business, labour, government and academia to improve productivity, quality and the quality of working life. Its main aim is to improve American productivity through the transfer of knowledge and best practices. APQC's focus is primarily in the field of benchmarking.

The Process Classification Framework was developed by the APQC in conjunction with Arthur Anderson in 1991 to facilitate process improvement.

Principles

When benchmarking, organizations often have problems identifying the processes to target in partner organizations, as processes are often named differently and have different scopes from organization to organization. The Process Classification Framework was developed as a simple form of 'translator' so that areas of interest could be identified during benchmarking activities.

By breaking down an organization's activities into a number of common processes, it is easier to compare 'like for like' areas and to see where processes vary significantly.

Approach

The main aims of the approach are to:

- encourage organizations to see their activities from a process rather than a functional viewpoint;
- encourage 'out of the box' thinking, where processes from different industries are adopted to advance an organization;
- help organizations to understand their processes better;
- help organizations to reach out across industry boundaries to communicate and share information;
- classify information in various forms.

The framework covers 13 top-level processes and is split into two sections:

- seven 'Operating' processes;
- six 'Management and Support' processes.

Each top-level process breaks down into a number of sub-processes, which themselves are sub-divided into a number of lower-level processes. The top-level processes are shown schematically below.

Top-level operating processes

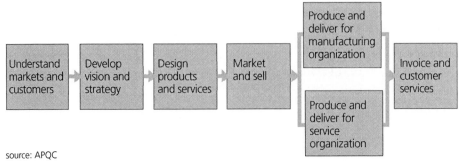

source: APQC

Top-level management and support processes

- Develop and manage human resources.
- Manage information.
- Manage financial and physical resources.
- Execute environmental management.
- Manage external relationships.
- Manage improvement and change (Source: APQC).

Although designed for benchmarking activities, the Process Classification Framework is an excellent aid to identifying an organization's processes for other purposes. These include process analysis as part of continuous improvement or BPR activities, and identifying process interfaces within and across departments. It is an extremely valuable aid when preparing an ISO 9001 system.

Process Management

How to use

Factor	Comments				
Link to ISO 9001	MR ✓	RM ✓	PR ✓	M&A ✓	Imp ✓
Scope of use	All types of organization Both manufacturing and service Function				
Degree of change in systems	Varies, depending on degree of change required				
Degree of change to people	Varies, depending on degree of change required				
Level of benefit	Varies, depending on degree of change required				
Level of involvement	Inclusive				
Maturity level	Beginner, experienced and world-class				
Timescale	It can take over 12 months to get a good understanding of process management and to see the first benefits				
Level of investment	Depends on improvement method used				
How to implement	Evolution or project				

Background

Process Management lies at the heart of all the business improvement models. It involves selecting, understanding, improving and continuously monitoring the performance of an organization's processes. Applicable to all organizations, Process Management is often a difficult area to implement without expert advice and support.

By mastering the management of critical processes it is possible to increase both effectiveness and efficiency, bringing higher stakeholder satisfaction and lower costs and often leading to the delivery of an organization's strategic objectives.

Process Management also gives many other internal benefits, typically:

- enhanced teamworking;
- better communication across functional areas;
- greater flexibility;
- increased staff satisfaction.

Principles

There are several principles to Process Management and these relate to way that processes are designed and operated. All processes have a purpose, receive inputs and, through a number of activities, transform the inputs into something more valuable in the form of outputs:

- **Process purpose:** what it is designed to achieve.
- **Inputs:** what the process transforms. They can be physical objects, such as iron bars, or information.
- **Outputs:** can also be either physical objects or information such as the cost of the service.
- **Added value:** when the work on the information or physical objects is complete, it must become more valuable to one of the stakeholders.

There are other factors that play a part in a process:

- **Controls:** the conditions under which the process must be operated. They may be external, such as health and safety legislation, or internal, such as procedures or performance measures.
- **Resources:** the inputs that do not change during the operation of the process. People, equipment and information are all forms of resources.
- **Process capability:** a measure of what the process may achieve. Take the process of hand-folding a piece of paper. A piece of A4 paper cannot be folded more than about eight times and it takes at least five seconds to perform the operation.

Approach

This approach is split into five phases.

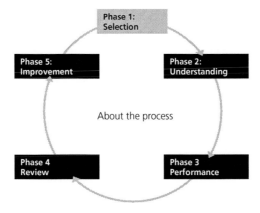

Phase 1: process selection

Agree a small number of business-critical processes upon which to focus. This is often achieved by considering the strategic objectives of the organization and identifying those processes that have a major impact on their achievement, and/or those that have most opportunity for improvement.

Phase 2: process understanding

Define the selected process or processes. This involves agreeing the purpose of the process, its scope, inputs, outputs, controls and resources. These factors are contained in the ICOR nomenclature:

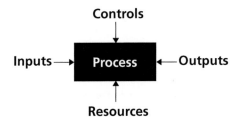

Phase 3: process performance

Research and gather historical performance data in preparation for the review of the performance of the process. This includes both factual and perceptual data as well as targets and benchmarks.

Phase 4: process review

Review the actual performance of the process against the targets and any external comparisons in order to establish improvement priorities. The targets provide a measure of performance against planned performance and the benchmarks a measure of performance against potential performance.

Phase 5: process improvement

Select the most appropriate method for delivering the process improvement. This could be a continuous improvement approach, or a re-engineering approach if a step change is required.

Self-assessment

How to use

Factor	Comments				
Link to ISO 9001	MR ✓	RM	PR	M&A ✓	Imp ✓
Scope of use	All types of organization Both manufacturing and service Function, division or organization				
Degree of change in systems	Small				
Degree of change to people	Small				
Level of benefit	Medium				
Level of involvement	Inclusive				
Maturity level	All, but the approach used will vary				
Timescale	Less than 3 months or 6–12 months depending on approach taken				
Level of investment	Medium to low				
How to implement	Project				

Background

The growth of self-assessment can be traced back to the earliest of the quality awards, the Deming Prize. This award promoted the need to review activities prior to the examination for the award.

The goals of Total Quality Management (TQM), customer satisfaction, continuous improvement and organizational excellence, are dynamic targets. They do not have a pre-fixed level. An organization must, therefore, be able to assess its current total quality performance against its past performance. This requires a rigorous self-assessment process and a suitable Total Quality framework to do it with. Thousands of organizations across the world are now using self-assessment on a regular basis. Self-assessment is not only a means of measuring continuous improvement; it also provides an excellent opportunity for integrating TQM into normal business activity.

To compete in today's aggressive business environment, organizations must deliver ever-greater value to their customers. Increasingly, leading organizations are turning to business improvement models to help them achieve their goals. The principles behind these models are simple – an organization will be profitable and grow if its products and services meet its customers' existing requirements as well as anticipate customers' future requirements. Products and services delivered through business processes must be continuously reviewed and improved by well-motivated and trained staff. This may be viewed as a business 'health check'.

Principles

Staff need to be actively involved in process improvement activities in order to improve the organization's effectiveness, efficiency and responsiveness. Self-assessment involves people in the regular and systematic review of their processes and results.

The process of self-assessment offers an organization an opportunity to identify clearly its strengths and improvement opportunities. It also enables an organization to focus valuable improvement resource where it is most effective, as well as enabling the progress of TQM programmes to be monitored.

Approach

There are many ways to conduct a self-assessment and the actual way chosen will depend on the objectives. There are essentially six basic approaches, which are summarized in the table below. There is also the option to take a 'hybrid' approach where a mixture of the approaches is used.

Approach	Description	When to use
Discussion group	Group meeting where a facilitator leads a discussion on the performance of the organization against the quality model.	In the early stages when senior managers have not experienced the full benefit of the approach. Very useful for communicating the principles and getting involvement.
Software-based questionnaire	Completion of a software-based questionnaire that allows a team to reach consensus on an organization's strengths and areas for improvement.	A team of senior managers with little prior knowledge of the Excellence Model may use a software programme such as BQF's Snapshot. It also provides information about approaches in other organizations. This is a good method to get the senior team on board and establish commitment to some early improvement action.
Surveys and questionnaires	Collection of people's perceptions by the completion of a survey or questionnaire. A typical questionnaire would have 100 questions.	To get wide involvement in the self-assessment process throughout all levels of the organization. Quick and simple to use.

Business Improvement Approaches

Approach	Description	When to use
Interviews	A facilitator collects self-assessment information by interviewing individuals (eg managers) and groups (eg work-level focus groups).	When senior manager time is at a premium or when visiting a manager's place of work to collect information can enhance the self-assessment. The focus groups are normally used to compare managers' perceptions of the current situation with the perceptions of other staff.
Matrices	The organization's current position is established by comparing evidence (and/or perceptions) against a number of statements, each with its own score. These statements are designed around scoring criteria. There may be 5–10 statements per criterion.	This approach is very simple and easy to perform. Its main advantage is that it is based on the scoring systems for the quality models, so it addresses the philosophy of business excellence as opposed to conformance to the criteria.
Pro formas	Completion of the self-assessment by collecting evidence on a pre-prepared form. There is normally one page for every criterion. The form also completes the assessment for the criterion by having a space for 'Strengths', 'Areas for improvement' and the score.	A natural progression from the simple techniques when the organization has started to recognize the benefits of self-assessment. The approach takes longer but returns higher quality feedback and a more accurate scoring profile.
Award style	The self-assessment mirrors the application for a quality award, which would require the compilation of a 75-page submission document. Trained, experienced, external assessors may be used as part of the approach. It may also include site visits to clarify and verify the 'application'.	Most suitable for organizations with at least three years' experience of conducting self-assessments. Although it is resource-intensive and can take six months to complete, this method provides extensive feedback highly suited for use in both strategic and business planning. It also allows a more accurate comparison with other organizations.

source: Porter and Tanner 2003

It should be noted that these approaches vary in a number of ways:

- the level of involvement of the managers and staff;
- the data collection methodology (eg, the balance between perceptions and facts);

- the time taken and level of resource required;
- the accuracy of the 'score';
- the richness of the feedback.

Despite these variations, there are basically eight steps in the self-assessment process:

source: Porter and Tanner 2003

1. Choose a framework

The framework or quality model on which the assessment is based will depend on a number of things, but the framework is likely to be the Baldrige Model, EFQM Excellence Model or a hybrid model specific to an organization. The assessment could also be based on ISO 9001, now that its perspective is one of *assessment* rather than *audit*.

2. Form the assessment team

As with any project, the selection, motivation and education of the project team members will be key to its success. It is also important for the team to take ownership of the project plan.

3. Collect the information

This step will vary enormously depending on the approach taken. The table above gives guidance on the best approach for a given situation.

4. Assessment and scoring

The level of sophistication for this step will also be dependent on the approach. At one extreme, with the simple scoring approaches, people will be asked, 'What do you think the score should be?' At the other extreme, with an award-style assessment, an independent assessor team may spend up to two days critically examining the evidence. The same applies to the identification of the 'Strengths' and 'Areas for Improvement'.

5. Consensus

Consensus is when a group meets to agree on the feedback from the assessment. With approaches such as the Discussion group and Matrices, the consensus is often an integral part of the process. With the other approaches there is likely to be a separate session to agree the assessment.

6. Site visit

This step is most appropriate for approaches such as the award-style assessment. After assessing the submission document and reaching consensus, the assessors may conduct a site visit to clarify and verify what they have read in the submission. It is normal for the feedback to be modified and the self-assessment re-scored on the basis of the visit's findings.

This step is particularly appropriate if an independent team has conducted the assessment. It is also valuable when there is a need to improve the accuracy of the feedback – there is nothing better than seeing the organization in action.

7. Feedback

The final output from the assessment will be feedback, normally in the form of a feedback report. This is a record of the self-assessment and will form the basis of the action planning. A typical feedback report will contain a summary of the main findings from the self-assessment, detailed 'Strengths' and 'Areas for Improvement', and a scoring profile.

8. Action planning

The output of the self-assessment is normally used in two main ways:

- to compile an improvement plan based on the 'Areas for Improvement'. This improvement plan may or may not be integrated into the business planning process;
- for strategic planning purposes. The self-assessment provides information that may be used by the senior managers to support the strategic decisions that are taken.

A general observation is that the more experienced an organization is with self-assessment, the more likely it is to use the feedback for strategic purposes. There is high risk in making strategic decisions on limited information, and only experienced organizations tend to invest the time and effort into the more resource-intensive self-assessment approaches that deliver information of high quality.

Six Sigma

How to use

Factor	Comments				
Link to ISO 9001	MR ✓	RM ✓	PR ✓	M&A ✓	Imp ✓
Scope of use	All types of organization Both manufacturing and service Organization				
Degree of change in systems	Medium				
Degree of change to people	Medium				
Level of benefit	Large				
Level of involvement	Fully inclusive				
Maturity level	Beginner, experienced and world-class				
Timescale	Over 12 months				
Level of investment	High, due to training costs				
How to implement	Programme				

Background

Six Sigma has been used the world over and many organizations testify to its pivotal role in their success. Well-known examples of Six Sigma organizations include Motorola, General Electric, AlliedSignal (now Honeywell), ABB, Lockheed Martin, Polaroid, Sony, Honda, American Express, Ford, Lear Corporation and Solectron.

The Motorola Company developed Six Sigma as a concept and aim. Motorola defined Six Sigma as 'a measure of goodness -- the capability of a process to produce perfect work'. Motorola had a goal of improving all products, goods as well as services, by an order of magnitude (eg, a factor of 10) within five years. This provided an important focus on the improvement rate and, in particular, that simply 'better' may not be sufficient, but that the critical issue is being *sufficiently better expeditiously*. Six Sigma clearly focused resources at Motorola, including human effort, on reducing variation in processes: manufacturing, administrative, and all other processes.

Motorola launched the Six Sigma programme in 1987 and signs of significant success quickly became apparent. From 1987 to 1997, Motorola achieved a fivefold growth in sales, with profits climbing nearly 20 per cent per year, cumulative savings at $US14 billion and stock price gains compounded to an annual rate of 21.3 per cent. Motorola was also cited as the first winner of America's Malcolm Baldrige National Quality Award in 1988.

Principles

The Six Sigma strategy is a disciplined methodology for improving organizations' process capability. It is based on extremely rigorous data gathering and statistical analysis to identify sources of variation and ways of reducing them.

Sigma is a statistical measure related to the capability of the process, that is, its ability to produce non-defective products/units/parts. In statistical jargon, sigma is a measure of process variation referred to as the standard deviation and Six Sigma implies the occurrence of defects at a rate of 3.4 defects per million opportunities (DPMO) for defects to arise.

It is possible to calibrate the 'cost of quality' or, more accurately, the 'cost of poor quality' (CPQ) with the sigma level at which processes perform. Six Sigma performance levels are generally considered to be world class, with the CPQ being less than 1 per cent of sales. Compare this to the lower sigma performance levels:

Sigma level	CPQ range	DPMO rate (%)
3	66,807	25–40
4	6,210	15–25
5	233	5–15

The main focus of Six Sigma is on defect reduction. But the benefits of such a reduction are many-fold, including improved customer satisfaction, reduced operating costs and increased efficiency.

Approach

The Six-Sigma breakthrough strategy involves a 'define-measure-analyse-improve-control' (DMAIC) methodology, which is applied to an organization's key business processes.

Phase 1. Define

Define the scope and goals of the improvement programme in terms of customer requirements and the process that delivers these requirements. The process to be improved is defined in terms of its inputs, outputs, controls and resources.

Phase 2. Measure

Measure the current process performance – input, output and process – and calculate the sigma metric for both short and longer-term process capability.

Phase 3. Analyse

Identify the gap between the current and desired performance, prioritize problems and identify their root causes. This phase may also include benchmarking the process outputs, products or services against recognized benchmark standards of performance. Depending upon the performance gap found, the organization will decide whether to improve or redesign the existing process.

Phase 4. Improve

Generate the improvement solutions to fix the problems and prevent them from recurring, so that the required financial and other performance goals are met. The organization will need to find new ways to do things to the quality, cost and time standards required by the performance improvement goals.

Phase 5. Control

Implement the improved process in a way that 'holds the gains'. Standards of operation will be documented in systems such as ISO 9001 and standards of performance will be established using techniques such as Statistical Process Control (SPC). After a 'running-in' period, calculate the process capability again to establish whether the performance gains are being sustained. Repeat the cycle if further performance shortfalls are identified.

Applying Six Sigma means that efficient, often statistical, techniques are used in a systematic way to reduce variation and improve processes. There is a focus on results, including customer-related ones that lead to enhanced marketplace performance and hence improved bottom-line financial results. Appropriately configured and deployed Six Sigma programmes may be highly consistent with the results-orientation underlying various international quality awards, such as the European Excellence Award and Malcolm Baldrige National Quality Award.

Building a Six Sigma culture and infrastructure

A key feature of a successful Six Sigma culture is the creation of an infrastructure that supports and resources performance improvement. Six Sigma programmes involve major investment and must deliver bottom-line results. There are 10 key features that characterize a successful Six Sigma culture:

1. Committed leadership.
2. Strategic alignment.
3. A cadre of change leaders.
4. Customer and market focus.
5. Bottom-line benefits.
6. Process approach.
7. Obsession with measurement.
8. Continuous innovation.
9. Organizational learning.
10. Continuous reinforcement.

Statistical Process Control (SPC)

How to use

Factor	Comments				
Link to ISO 9001	MR	RM	PR	M&A ✓	Imp
Scope of use	All types of organization Both manufacturing and service, but most success has been with manufacturing units Organization				
Degree of change in systems	Medium				
Degree of change to people	Medium				
Level of benefit	Large				
Level of involvement	Fully inclusive				
Maturity level	Beginner, experienced and world-class				
Timescale	Over 12 months				
Level of investment	Medium, due to training costs				
How to implement	Programme				

Background

Statistical process control was at the heart of the Japanese quality revolution in the 1950s. Often avoided due to its perceived heavy reliance on complex mathematical equations, SPC is all about having more confidence in the quality of a process output.

SPC is a problem solving approach. In reality it is '10 per cent statistics and 90 per cent management action'. Like Kaizen, Six Sigma and Total Quality Management, SPC has a need for quality improvement leadership and a systematic approach.

SPC has been used mainly in manufacturing industry, although it does have some application in service industries. The main problem with its use in the service sector is that this sector does not produce tangible objects with a physical specification. Despite this the principles remain the same. For further reading on the application of SPC to service industries, see Appendix 2.

Principles

SPC recognizes that not all items produced will be the same. There is always going to be some variation around the output of a process with a minimum, maximum and average. If we plot the dimensions of the item against the number obtained it is likely that we will see the following 'normal' curve:

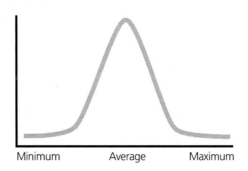

| Minimum | Average | Maximum |

Taking a sample of the output, it is possible to predict what the minimum, maximum and average dimensions will be. If the minimum and maximum are within the specification laid down, then the process is 'in control'.

The main principle is therefore, 'Have we made it ok?' This involves asking:

- Are we in control? Do we have consistency?
- Are we capable? Are we able to produce conforming product all of the time?
- Can we continue to produce conforming products? Do we continue to be in control?
- Have we done the job right?
- *Could we do the job better?*

Approach

Establish control charts for the output being measured. Take five parts from production at regular intervals. Measure the parts and calculate the average and the 'range', which is the largest minus the smallest reading.

Plot the results on the control chart. The central area in the example control chart below represents results where the process is in control. The lightly shaded areas provide a warning that the process may be going 'out of control' and the outer areas show where the process is 'out of control'. This indicates that products are likely to be out of specification.

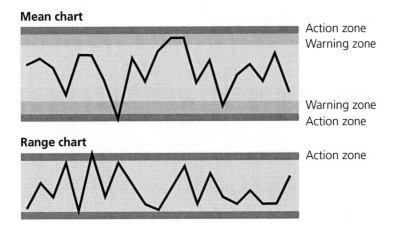

Mean chart

Action zone
Warning zone

Warning zone
Action zone

Range chart

Action zone

Under normal conditions, the results will vary for many understandable reasons. These might be due to small process changes, differences in materials and errors in the measurements taken. These differences are said to be due to 'Common causes of variation'.

Sometimes there will be a major change in the process. This could be due to the use of incorrect or reject parts, or an operational change such as that caused by incorrect maintenance. When this happens the process is likely to go out of control and register in the outer area of the control chart. Such changes are said to be due to 'Special causes'.

Theory of Constraints

How to use

Factor	Comments				
Link to ISO 9001	MR	RM	PR	M&A	Imp
		✓	✓		✓
Scope of use	All types of organization Both manufacturing and service Function				
Degree of change in systems	Medium to small				
Degree of change to people	Medium				
Level of benefit	Medium				
Level of involvement	Inclusive				
Maturity level	Experienced or world-class				
Timescale	Over 12 months				
Level of investment	Low to medium				
How to implement	Evolution				

Background

Based on Deming's concept of 'profound knowledge' and systems thinking, the Theory of Constraints was developed by Eliyahu Goldratt based on his experience of manufacturing. The theory is based on his book, *The Goal*, which was first published in 1984.

Goldratt examines the nature of science and education. He sees science as being the use of a minimum number of assumptions to explain the many phenomena of nature. Education or learning, on the other hand, is delivered through the process of deduction. The consequence is that his technique recognizes the use of assumptions to describe activity and deduction to predict future behaviour.

The Theory of Constraints (TOC) is described as a systems approach to continuous improvement. It is a collection of systems principles and tools or methods for improving the overall system performance.

Principles

Deming's 'profound knowledge' comes from:

- an understanding of the theory of knowledge;
- knowledge of variation;
- an understanding of psychology;
- appreciation of systems.

TOC rests on the assumption that managers and/or organizations know their real purpose and the goal they are trying to achieve. Unfortunately, this is not always the case. No manager can hope to succeed, however, without knowing three things:

1. what the ultimate goal is;
2. where he or she currently stands in relation to that goal;
3. the magnitude and direction of the change needed to move from the status quo to where he or she wants to be (the goal).

The Theory of Constraints has a number of principles:

Systems as chains

This is crucial to TOC. If systems function like chains, weakest links can be found and strengthened.

Local vs system optima

Because of interdependence and variation, the optimum performance of a system as a whole is not the same as the sum of all the local optima. If all the components of a system are performing at their maximum level, the system as whole will not necessarily be performing at its best.

Cause and effect

All systems operate in an environment of cause and effect. Something causes something else to happen. This cause-and-effect phenomenon can be very complicated, especially in complex systems.

Undesirable effects and core problems

Nearly all of the undesirable effects seen in a system are not problems, but indicators. They are the resultant effects of underlying causes. Eliminating undesirable effects gives a false sense of security. Identifying and eliminating the core problem not only eliminates all the undesirable effects that issue from it, but it prevents them from returning.

Solution deterioration

An optimal solution deteriorates over time, as the system's environment changes. A process of ongoing improvement is necessary to update and maintain the efficiency (and effectiveness) of a solution. Inertia is the worst enemy of a process of ongoing improvement. The attitude that 'We've solved that problem, no need to revisit it' damages continuous improvement efforts.

Physical vs policy constraints

Most of the constraints in systems originate from policies, not physical things. Physical constraints are relatively easy to identify and break. Policy constraints are much more difficult, but they normally result in a much larger degree of system improvement than elimination of a physical constraint.

Ideas are NOT solutions

The best ideas in the world never realize their potential unless they are implemented. And most great ideas fail in the implementation stage.

Approach

Goldratt developed five sequential 'focusing' steps to concentrate improvement effort on the component that is capable of producing the most positive impact on the system.

Step 1. Identify the system constraint

What part of the system constitutes the weakest link? Is it physical or is it a policy?

Step 2. Decide how to exploit the constraint

This means wringing every bit of capability out of the constraining component as it currently exists. In other words, getting the most out of the constraint without committing to potentially expensive changes or upgrades.

Step 3. Subordinate everything else

The rest of the system needs to be adjusted to a 'setting' that will enable a constraint to operate at maximum effectiveness. This may mean 'de-tuning' some parts of the system, while 'revving up' others. Then evaluate the results: is the constraint still constraining the system's performance? If not, move ahead to Step 5. If it is, continue with Step 4.

Step 4. Elevate the constraint

This step considers the idea of major changes to the existing system – reorganization, divestiture, capital improvements, or other substantial system modifications. It can involve considerable investment in time, energy, money, or other resources, so this step should only be taken if it is not possible to break the constraint in the first three steps. 'Elevating' the constraint means taking whatever action is required to eliminate the constraint. When this step is completed the constraint is broken.

Step 5. Go back to Step 1, but beware of 'inertia'

It is important to keep on looking for and breaking other constraints, and not to become complacent. Because of interdependency and variation, each subsequent change made to the system will have new effects on the constraints already broken. They may need to be revisited and updated too.

The Five Focusing Steps have a direct relationship with the three management questions pertaining to change: what to change, what to change to, and how to cause change. They explain how to answer those questions.

Total Productive Maintenance

How to use

Factor	Comments				
Link to ISO 9001	MR	RM	PR	M&A	Imp
	✓	✓	✓	✓	
Scope of use	All types of organization Almost exclusively manufacturing Manufacturing function				
Degree of change in systems	Small				
Degree of change to people	Large				
Level of benefit	Large to medium depending on the success of implementation				
Level of involvement	Fully inclusive				
Maturity level	Beginners, experienced or world-class				
Timescale	Over 12 months				
Level of investment	Medium				
How to implement	Programme				

Background

Total Productive Maintenance (TPM) is a proven approach to continuous improvement that was developed in Japan. More than 700 successful factories worldwide are using the approach.

Being factory-centred, the approach examines and improves the relationship between operator and machine. It is results-focused with the main target being the removal of the main obstacles to efficient performance.

The approach is a very systematic programme, which takes around two to five years to implement. A key component is staff training, mainly shop-floor workers. They work in small cross-functional teams to implement improvements.

Such is the popularity of the approach that there is a Japanese society that promotes it and provides training. The society promotes a recognition scheme allowing organizations to reach particular 'levels' and there is also an annual award process.

Business Improvement Approaches

A number of TPM benefits have been noted, including improvements in productivity, quality, costs, delivery, safety, the environment and employee morale.

Principles

The principles of TPM are represented by the 'TPM Pillars'. These 'pillars' are similar to the components of Total Quality Management and other continuous improvement approaches. As expected, a maintenance theme runs throughout the approach. 'Autonomous maintenance' requires operators to perform simple maintenance on their own machinery and 'Effective maintenance' ensures minimum equipment downtime.

TPM knowledge/information

- Autonomous maintenance
- Focused improvement
- Effective maintenance
- Quality maintenance
- Early management
- Training for operation and maintenance skills
- TPM in the office
- Safety, hygiene and environmental activities

Approach

The approach to TPM is systematic and goes through different phases as the implementation progresses. A typical implementation plan would be as follows.

Preparation

Step 1.   Formally announce decision to introduce TPM.
Step 2.   TPM introductory education and publicity campaign.
Step 3.   Create a TPM promotion organization.
Step 4.   Establish basic TPM policy and goals.
Step 5.   Create a master plan to implement TPM.

Introduction/Roll-out

Step 6.   Kick off TPM initiatives.

Implementation

Step 7.   Build a corporate constitution to maximize productive effectiveness:
- focused improvement;
- autonomous maintenance;
- effective maintenance;
- training.

Step 8.   Early management.

Step 9.   Quality maintenance (ISO 9001).

Step 10. TPM in administration.

Step 11. Safety, hygiene, and environment.

Stabilization

Step 12. Full TPM implementation and raise levels.

Total Quality Management (TQM)

How to use

Factor	Comments				
Link to ISO 9001	MR ✓	RM ✓	PR ✓	M&A ✓	Imp ✓
Scope of use	All types of organization Both manufacturing and service Division or organization				
Degree of change in systems	Small				
Degree of change to people	Large				
Level of benefit	Large to medium depending on the success of implementation				
Level of involvement	Fully inclusive				
Maturity level	Beginner				
Timescale	Over 12 months				
Level of investment	High				
How to implement	Programme				

Background

TQM is based on Kaizen, the Japanese philosophy of continuous improvement. Interest in Japanese methods increased in the late 1960s when Western organizations faced competition from a part of the world that had long been known for producing shoddy, cheap goods. Suddenly there was a new competitor that was not only lower priced, but also produced goods of higher quality and specification. The revolution had been led by two Americans who received no airtime for their ideas in their country of origin, Dr Deming and Dr Juran.

There are many approaches to implementing continuous improvement, each with their individual features. The approach advocated by Deming relates to leadership and the reduction in variation. Juran's approach, although still advocating the reduction in variation, focuses on the use of quality planning and improvement projects. Crosby (1979) made the terms 'conformance to requirements', 'prevention', 'zero defects' and 'price of non-conformance' his catchphrases.

The approach described here is the one attributed to John Oakland. It has been adopted by many UK organizations and the Department of Trade and Industry.

Principles

TQM is far wider in its application than just assuring product or service quality: it is a way of managing people and business processes to ensure complete customer satisfaction at every stage, internally and externally. TQM, combined with effective leadership, results in an organization doing things right, first time.

Processes are a key linkage between the enablers of *planning* (leadership driving policy and strategy, partnerships and resources), through *people* into the *performance* (measured by people, society, customers and key outcomes). These 'four Ps' form the basis of a model for TQM and provide the 'hard management necessities' to take organizations successfully into the 21st century.

We must not underestimate the importance of the three Cs – Culture, Communication and Commitment. A simple model for TQM is complete when these 'soft outcomes' are integrated into the four Ps framework to move organizations forward successfully.

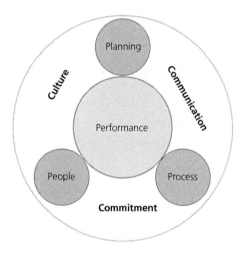

source: Oakland 2003

Approach

The task of implementing TQM can be daunting. The following is a list of Oakland's points that leaders should consider. They are a distillation of the various beliefs of many of the quality gurus, applied in a pragmatic way.

1. The organization needs a long-term **commitment** to continuous improvement.
2. Adopt the philosophy of zero errors/defects to change the **culture** to 'right first time'.
3. Train people to understand the **customer-supplier** relationships.
4. Do not buy products or services on price alone – look at the **total cost**.

---

5. Recognize that improvement of the **systems** must be managed.
6. Adopt modern methods of **supervising and training** – eliminate fear.
7. Eliminate barriers between departments by managing the **process** – improve **communication** and **teamwork**.
8. Eliminate goals without methods, standards based only on numbers, barriers to pride of workmanship, and fiction – get **facts** by studying **processes**.
9. Constantly educate and retrain – develop **experts** in the organization.
10. Develop a **systematic** approach to manage the implementation of TQM.

Oakland gives advice on organizational barriers that may be overcome by adopting TQM and asks the question, 'How many of these behaviours do you recognize in your organization?' These 'bad practices' are:

- Leaders not giving clear direction.
- Not understanding, or ignoring competitive positioning.
- Each department working only for itself.
- Trying to control people through systems.
- Confusing quality with grade.
- Accepting that a level of defects or errors is inevitable.
- Fire-fighting, reactive behaviour.
- The 'It's not my problem' attitude.

Glossary of terms

Abbreviation	Definition
APQC	American Productivity and Quality Center
ASQ	American Society for Quality
BPIR	Business Performance Improvement Review
BPR	Business Process Re-engineering
BQF	British Quality Foundation
BQSR	Better Quality Service Review
BSC	Balanced Score Card
CPQ	Cost of Poor Quality
CSF	Critical Success Factor
DMAIC	Define-Measure-Analyse-Improve-Control
DPMO	Defects Per Million Operations
EC*for*BE	European Centre for Business Excellence
EFQM	European Foundation for Quality Management
Evolution	Ongoing change with no predefined end point
FMEA	Failure Mode Effect Analysis
IiP	Investors in People
Imp	Improvement (ISO 9001 requirement)
IQA	Institute of Quality Assurance
ISO 9000	ISO 9000: Vocabulary
ISO 9001	ISO 9001: Requirements
ISO 9004	ISO 9004: Guidelines for Performance Improvement
JiT	Just in Time
KPI	Key Performance Indicator
M&A	Measurement and Analysis (ISO 9001 requirement)
MR	Management Responsibility (ISO 9001 requirement)
OEE	Overall Equipment Effectiveness
PCF	Process Classification Framework
PMF	Performance Measurement Framework
Poke Yoke	'Mistake proofing'
PR	Process Management (ISO 9001 requirement)
Programme	A combination of business improvement projects with a distinct beginning and end
Project	A business improvement activity with a distinct beginning and end
RADAR	Results, Approach, Deployment, Assessment and Review
RM	Resource Management (ISO 9001 requirement)
SME	Small – Medium Enterprises
SOP	Standard Operating Procedures
SPC	Statistical Process Control
TOC	Theory of Constraints
TPM	Total Productive Maintenance
TQM	Total Quality Management

Appendix 1
Where the approaches support the business improvement models

Where the approaches support ISO 9001

Approach[1]	Management responsibility	Resource management	Product realization[2]	Measurement and analysis	Improvement
Balanced Scorecards (BSC)	✓		✓	✓	✓
Benchmarking					✓
Best Value	✓		✓	✓	✓
Better Quality Service Reviews (BQSR)	✓		✓	✓	✓
Business Performance Improvement Review (BPIR)	✓	✓	✓		✓
Business Process Re-engineering (BPR)					✓
Charter Mark		✓	✓	✓	✓
Failure Mode Effect Analysis (FMEA)			✓	✓	✓
Investors in People (IiP)	✓	✓			✓
Kaizen/Continuous Improvement		✓	✓		✓
Kaizen Teams		✓	✓		✓
Lean Thinking			✓	✓	✓
Performance Measurement	✓		✓	✓	✓

Appendix 1

Approach[1]	Management responsibility	Resource management	Product realization[2]	Measurement and analysis	Improvement
Process Classification Framework (PCF)			✓		
Process Management	✓	✓	✓	✓	✓
Self-assessment	✓			✓	
Six Sigma	✓	✓	✓	✓	✓
Statistical Process Control (SPC)				✓	
Theory of Constraints		✓	✓	✓	✓
Total Productive Maintenance		✓	✓	✓	✓
Total Quality Management	✓	✓	✓	✓	✓

Note 1 Only the main linkages are shown.

Note 2 Product realization may be taken to include process management.

Where the approaches support the Baldrige Model

Approach[1]	Leadership	Strategic planning	Customer and market focus	Information and analysis	Human resource focus	Process management	Business results
Balanced Scorecards (BSC)	✓	✓	✓	✓	✓	✓	✓
Benchmarking		✓		✓		✓	✓
Best Value		✓	✓	✓		✓	✓
Better Quality Service Reviews (BQSR)	✓	✓	✓			✓	✓
Business Performance Improvement Review (BPIR)	✓	✓	✓	✓	✓	✓	✓
Business Process Re-engineering (BPR)						✓	
Charter Mark			✓	✓	✓	✓	✓
Failure Mode Effect Analysis (FMEA)	✓		✓			✓	
Investors in People (IiP)		✓		✓	✓		✓
Kaizen/Continuous Improvement			✓	✓	✓	✓	
Kaizen Teams						✓	✓

Appendix 1

Approach[1]	Leadership	Strategic planning	Customer and market focus	Information and analysis	Human resource focus	Process management	Business results
Lean Thinking	✓		✓		✓	✓	✓
Performance Measurement		✓	✓	✓		✓	✓
Process Classification Framework (PCF)						✓	
Process Management					✓	✓	✓
Self-assessment	✓	✓	✓	✓	✓	✓	✓
Six Sigma						✓	✓
Statistical Process Control (SPC)						✓	✓
Theory of Constraints						✓	✓
Total Productive Maintenance					✓	✓	✓
Total Quality Management					✓	✓	✓

Note 1 Only the main linkages are shown.

Where the approaches support the EFQM Excellence Model®

Approach[1]	Leadership	Policy and strategy	People	Partnerships and resources	Processes	Customer results	People results	Society results	Key performance results
Balanced Scorecards (BSC)		✓	✓		✓	✓	✓		✓
Benchmarking		✓			✓				✓
Best Value				✓	✓				✓
Better Quality Service Reviews (BQSR)		✓		✓	✓	✓			✓
Business Performance Improvement Review (BPIR)	✓	✓	✓	✓	✓	✓	✓	✓	✓
Business Process Re-engineering (BPR)			✓	✓	✓	✓			
Charter Mark			✓	✓	✓	✓	✓		
Failure Mode Effect Analysis (FMEA)					✓				

Appendix 1

Approach[1]	Leadership	Policy and strategy	People	Partnerships and resources	Processes	Customer results	People results	Society results	Key performance results
Investors in People (IiP)			✓				✓		✓
Kaizen/Continuous Improvement	✓		✓		✓	✓	✓		✓
Kaizen Teams			✓		✓	✓			✓
Lean Thinking				✓	✓	✓			✓
Performance Measurement		✓		✓	✓	✓	✓	✓	✓
Process Classification Framework (PCF)	✓	✓			✓				
Process Management		✓			✓	✓			
Self-assessment	✓	✓	✓	✓	✓		✓	✓	✓
Six Sigma					✓				✓
Statistical Process Control (SPC)					✓				✓

Appendix 1

Approach[1]	Leadership	Policy and strategy	People	Partnerships and resources	Processes	Customer results	People results	Society results	Key performance results
Theory of Constraints				✓	✓				✓
Total Productive Maintenance			✓	✓	✓	✓	✓	✓	✓
Total Quality Management			✓	✓	✓	✓	✓	✓	✓

Note 1 Only the main linkages are shown.

Appendix 2
Further information and reading

Balanced Scorecard

Kaplan, R S and Norton, D P (1992) 'The Balanced Scorecard. Measures that Drive Performance', *Harvard Business Review*, January – February

Kaplan, R S and Norton, D P (1996) *The Balanced Scorecard*, Harvard Business School Press, Boston

Kaplan, R S and Norton, D P (2001) *The Strategy Focused Organization*, Harvard Business School Press, Boston

The Malcolm Baldrige Award

www.quality.nist.gov

Hendricks, K B and Singhal, V R (1999) 'Don't count TQM out', *Quality Progress*, 32 (4) 35–42

Benchmarking

American Productivity and Quality Center (1993) *Benchmarking Management Guide*, Productivity Press, Houston

Camp, R C (1989) *Benchmarking*, ASQC, Milwaukee

Tanner, S J and Walker, R (2003) *The Benchmarking Roadmap*, European Centre for Business Excellence, Leeds

Better Quality Service Reviews (BQSR)

HMSO (1998) *Better Quality Services*, HMSO, London

Business Performance Improvement Review (BPIR)

ISO 9004:2000 *Guidelines for Performance Improvement*, www.bsi-global/bpir

Business Process Re-engineering (BPR)

Hammer, M and Champy, J (1993) *Reengineering the Corporation: A Manifesto for Business Revolution*, HarperBusiness, New York

Hammer, M and Stanton, S (1999) 'How Process Enterprises Really Work', *Harvard Business Review*, November – December

Charter Mark

www.chartermark.gov.uk

The EFQM Excellence Model®

www.efqm.org

www.quality-foundation.co.uk

The X Factor (1998) British Quality Foundation, London

The Model in Practice (2002) British Quality Foundation, London

European Centre *for* Business Excellence (1997) *Evaluating the operation of the model for self-assessment*, Leeds

European Foundation for Quality Management (2003) *The EFQM Excellence Model*, EFQM, Brussels

European Foundation for Quality Management (2003) *Assessing for Excellence*, EFQM, Brussels

Reed, D (1995) 'Public test on the award model', *UK Quality*, September

Failure Mode Effect Analysis (FMEA)

www.sti.nasa.gov

www.fmeainfocentre.com

Investors in People (IiP)

www.investorsinpeople.co.uk

ISO 9001: 2000, ISO 9000, ISO 9004

www.bsi-global.com

www.iso.ch

Kaizen/Continuous Improvement

Deming, W E (1994) *The New Economics*, 2nd edn, MIT, Cambridge, MA

Imai, M (1997) *Gemba Kaizen*, McGraw-Hill, New York

Oakland, J S (1993) *Total Quality Management*, 2nd edn, Butterworth-Heinemann, Oxford

Kaizen Teams

Laraia, A C, Moody, P E and Hall, R W (1999) *The Kaizen Blitz: Accelerating breakthroughs in productivity and performance*, Wiley, New York

Lean Thinking

Ballé, M (1994) *Systems Thinking*, McGraw-Hill, Maidenhead

Senge, P M (1993) *The Fifth Discipline – The art and practice of the learning organization*, Century Business, London

Womack, J P and Jones, D T (1996) *Lean Thinking*, Simon & Schuster, New York

Womack, J P, Jones, D T and Roos, D (1991) *The Machine that Changed the World*, Simon & Schuster, New York

Performance Measurement

Kaplan, R S and Norton, D P (1992) 'The Balanced Scorecard. Measures that Drive Performance', *Harvard Business Review*, January – February

Kaplan, R S and Norton, D P (1996) *The Balanced Scorecard*, Harvard Business School Press, Boston

Neely, N D (1998) *Measuring Business Performance*, Profile Books Ltd, London

Neely, N D, Adams, C and Kennerley, M (2002) *The Performance Prism: The scorecard for measuring and managing stakeholder relationships*, Financial Times/Prentice Hall, London

Process Classification Framework (PCF)

www.apqc.org

Process Management

Hammer, M (2001) *The Agenda*, Crown Business, New York

Harrington, H J (1991) *Business Process Improvement*, McGraw-Hill, New York

Oakland, J S (2003) *Total Quality Management. Text with cases*, 3rd edn, Butterworth-Heinemann, Oxford

Self-assessment

European Foundation for Quality Management (1999) *Assessing for Excellence*, EFQM, Brussels

Porter, L and Tanner, S J (2003) *Assessing Business Excellence*, 3rd edn, Butterworth-Heinemann, Oxford

Six Sigma

Chowdhury, S (2001) *The Power of Six Sigma*, Dearborn Trade, Chicago

Harry, M and Schroder, R (2000) *Six Sigma*, Doubleday, New York

Statistical Process Control (SPC)

Oakland, J S (2003) *Statistical Process Control*, 5th edn, Butterworth-Heinemann, Oxford

Wheeler (1993) *Understanding Variation*, SPC Press Inc, Knoxville

Theory of Constraints

Deming, W E (1994) *The New Economics*, 2nd edn, Massachusetts Institute for Technology, Cambridge, MA

Dettmer, H W (1997) *Goldratt's Theory of Constraints*, ASQ Press, Milwaukee

Goldratt, E.M (1992) *The Goal*, 2nd edn, North River Press, Great Barrington

Total Productive Maintenance

Basu, R and Wright, J T (1997) *Total Manufacturing Solutions*, Butterworth-Heinemann, Oxford

Takahashi, Y and Osada, T (1990) *Total Productive Maintenance*, Asian Productivity Organization, Tokyo

Total Quality Management (TQM)

www.dti.gov.uk/quality

Crosby, P (1979) *Quality is Free*, McGraw-Hill, New York

Deming, W E (1994) *The New Economics*, 2nd edn, Massachusetts Institute for Technology, Cambridge, MA

Deming, W E (1996) *Out of the Crisis*, MIT, Cambridge MA

Juran, J M (1992) *Juran on Quality by Design: The new steps for planning quality into goods and services*, The Free Press, New York

Oakland, J S (2003) *Total Quality Management. Text with cases*, 3rd edn, Butterworth-Heinemann, Oxford

Appendix 3
The European Centre for Business Excellence and BSI

The European Centre *for* Business Excellence

ECforBE is the research and education division of Oakland Consulting plc, operating in alliance with Leeds University Business School (LUBS) and several other universities across Europe. It provides an essential link between the academic and business worlds.

The Centre's main purpose is to develop both knowledge and capability within organizations with a focus on improving performance through knowledge into action. It does this by carrying out research and education activities that keep both Oakland Consulting plc and its clients on the frontiers of knowledge and thinking in their chosen areas of activity.

The growing reputation of the ECforBE has been founded on the publication of research reports and books such as:

The X-Factor (British Quality Foundation)
Designing Business Excellence
The Model in Practice (British Quality Foundation)
Evaluating the Use of the Business Excellence Model for Self-assessment

The Centre has also published research papers on subjects as diverse as benchmarking, business process re-engineering, self-assessment, people management and stress management in numerous refereed journals. Conference presentations and papers are regularly presented across the world, for example, at NFKL, EOQ, EFQM, SQCA, ASQ, and TQM conferences.

Research and special projects conducted on behalf of clients have included:

- Designing the material to support a web-based quality initiative for the DTI.
- Researching and designing the content and presentation for a web site for the Design Council.
- Producing case study material for BSI.
- Researching good practices for Oakland Consulting division clients.
- Conducting qualitative and quantitative research projects for both industry and academia.

Executive development and coaching form a major part of the ECforBE portfolio. In addition to developing and teaching modules on MBA and Masters in Management programmes at LUBS and other leading business schools throughout the world, the ECforBE also plays an active role developing executives challenged with achieving their organization's strategic objectives by delivering tailored programmes to improve their skills and competences. Executive coaching allows support for change to be provided in the workplace.

The European Centre *for* Business Excellence can be contacted on: Tel: +44 (0)113 244 9434, Fax: +44 (0)113 233 1988, E-mail: contactus@ecforbe.com, or visit: www.ecforbe.com.

BSI Management Systems

BSI Management Systems is part of the BSI group of companies. BSI is a major contributor to the International Standards Organization and works globally with sectoral experts, top companies and governments to develop frameworks for establishing best practice in an ever-increasing range of activities.

BSI Management Systems uses its vast experience in management strategy, gained through working with all sizes of organizations in every sector, to help clients increase their competitive advantage by:

- improving effectiveness;
- reducing costs, increasing customer focus and satisfaction; and
- encouraging commitment to continual improvement.

BSI Management Systems' role is that of an 'inside' facilitator, working closely with clients to improve their competitive position.

BSI Management Systems can be contacted on: Tel: +44 (0)20 8996 7720 (Europe, Middle East and Africa); Tel: +1 (703) 437 9000 (Americas); Tel: +852 2147 9891 (Asia Pacific) or visit: www.bsi-global.com.